THE EARLY
HUMAN WORLD

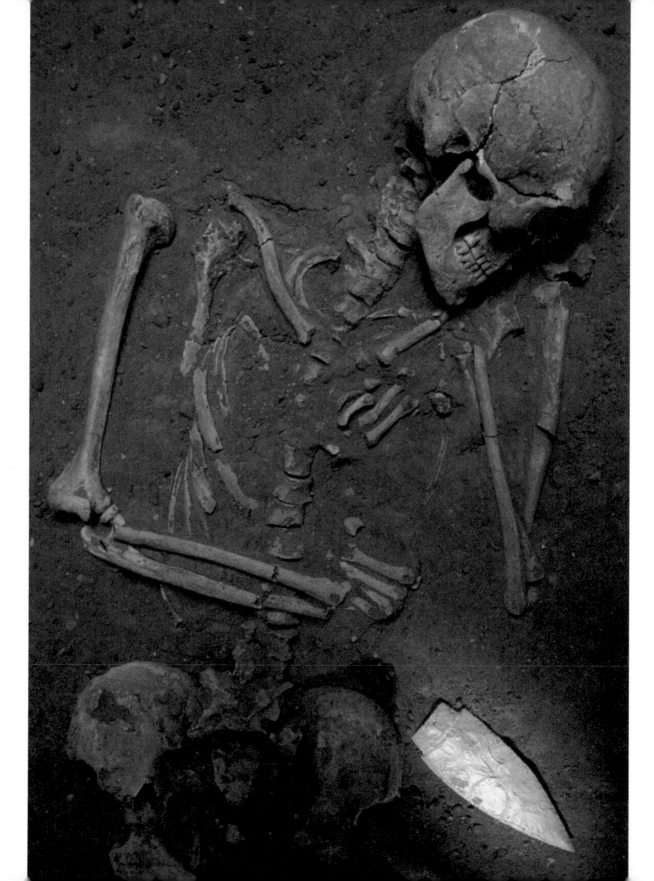

THE WORLD IN ANCIENT TIMES

RONALD MELLOR &
AMANDA H. PODANY

GENERAL EDITORS

THE EARLY HUMAN WORLD

Peter Robertshaw & Jill Rubalcaba

OXFORD

UNIVERSITY PRESS

*For Denyse and Dan, our true partners in all things.
And for the men and women whose passion for digging up the past
has unearthed how we,* Homo sapiens sapiens, *came to be.*

OXFORD
UNIVERSITY PRESS

Oxford   New York
Auckland   Bangkok   Buenos Aires   Cape Town   Chennai
Dar es Salaam   Delhi   Hong Kong   Istanbul   Karachi   Kolkata
Kuala Lumpur   Madrid   Melbourne   Mexico City   Mumbai
Nairobi   São Paulo   Shanghai   Taipei   Tokyo   Toronto

Published by Oxford University Press, Inc.
198 Madison Avenue, New York, New York, 10016
www.oup.com

Oxford is a registered trademark of Oxford University Press

Design: Stephanie Blumenthal
Layout: Alexis Siroc
Cover design and logo: Nora Wertz

Library of Congress Cataloging-in-Publication Data
Robertshaw, Peter.
The early human world / by Peter Robertshaw and Jill Rubalcaba.
p. cm.
ISBN 0-19-516157-2
ISBN 0-19-518213-8 (California edition)
ISBN 0-19-522242-3 (9-volume set)
1. Human beings-Origin. 2. Fossil hominids. 3. Prehistoric
peoples. 4. Agriculture, Prehistoric. I. Rubalcaba, Jill. II. Title.

GN281.R63 2005
930--dc22
                                                          2004009732

9 8 7 6 5 4 3 2 1

Printed in the United States on acid-free paper.

On the cover: The Neandertal skull from Wadi Amud, Israel, is about 60,000 years old, and the rock painting from Tassili n'Ajjer, Algeria, is about 4,000 years old.
Frontispiece: A ceremonial flint knife lies beside a skeleton buried about 4,600 years ago at Remedello Sotto, in northern Italy.

**RONALD MELLOR &
AMANDA H. PODANY**

GENERAL EDITORS

CONTENTS

A 💬 *marks each chapter's primary sources—ancient writings, fossils, and artifacts that "speak" to us from the past.*

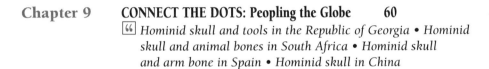

CAST OF CHARACTERS

Amesbury Archer, alias the king of Stonehenge, 4,300 years ago • A wealthy man buried in southern England during the Early Bronze Age

Ardipithecus ramidus kadabba (ar-dee-PITH-eh-kus RAM-eh-dus kad-ABBA), 5.8–4.3 million years ago • The earliest known hominid, found in Ethiopia; some scientists think that this hominid should be named *Ardipithecus kadabba*

Australopithecus afarensis (ahs-trul-o-PITH-eh-kus a-far-EN-sis), 3.9–3 million years ago • The species of early hominid that made the Laetoli footprints; Lucy is a member of this species

Australopithecus boisei (ahs-trul-o-PITH-eh-kus BOYZ-ee-eye), 2–1 million years ago • An East African hominid with large jaws and teeth that ate hard food, such as nuts and seeds; also known as *Paranthropus boisei*

Australopithecus garhi (ahs-trul-o-PITH-eh-kus GAR-hee), 2.5 million years ago • Newly discovered species of hominid found in Ethiopia by Tim White and his colleagues

Australopithecus robustus (ahs-trul-o-PITH-eh-kus roh-BUST-us), 1.9–1 million years ago • Sturdily built hominid in Southern Africa that became extinct, also known as *Paranthropus robustus*

Barker, **Graeme**, b. 1946 • English professor of archaeology who led an expedition to the Sahara Desert in 2002

Bar-Yosef, **Ofer** (OH-fer), b. 1937 • Archaeologist and professor of anthropology at Harvard University who investigates the origins of agriculture and modern humans

Binford, **Lewis**, b. 1930 • American archaeologist who has studied the lifestyles of ancient and modern hunters and gatherers

Chimpanzees at Burgers' Zoo • A captive colony of common chimpanzees (*Pan trogolodytes*), being observed by scholars

Clovis People, 13,200–12,900 years ago • Hunting-and-gathering people in North America who used distinctive spear points to kill mammoths and other big game

Cro-Magnons (CROH-MAN-yon), about 35,000–10,000 years ago • The first modern humans in Europe, named after an archaeological site in France

Darwin, **Charles**, 1809–1882 • British naturalist who is best known for his theories on evolution and natural selection

Deacon, **Hilary**, b. 1936 • South African archaeologist who has excavated many important Stone Age sites in southern Africa

Dillehay, **Thomas** (DILL-uh-hay), b. 1947 • Professor of anthropology at the University of Kentucky whose excavations at Monte Verde, Chile, have provided new information on the first people to come to the Americas

Duarte, **Cidália** (DWAR-tay, SEE-dahl-ee-ah), Active since 1995 • Portuguese archaeologist who excavated the skeleton of the Kid while she was still a student

Goodall, Jane (GOOD-awl), b. 1934 • Goodall has dedicated most of her life to the study and conservation of chimpanzees. As a child, she loved to read books about animals; she decided that she wanted to go to Africa to study them when she grew up

Haile-Selassie, Yohannes (HI-lee-sell-ASS-ee, YO-hahn), b. 1962 • Ethiopian anthropologist and finder of the earliest known hominid

Heyerdahl, Thor (HI-yer-dahl, tor), 1914–2002 • Norwegian explorer and archaeologist who made long ocean voyages on simple boats and rafts

Hodder, Ian, b. 1948 • British archaeologist who directs the excavations at Çatalhöyük

hominid • A member of the family of mammals named Hominidae. Humans are the only surviving species of this family. Extinct hominids include all the species discussed in this book that habitually walked on two legs

Hominid gang • A team of Kenyan fossil hunters led by Kamoya Kimeu who have made many important discoveries on expeditions directed by the Leakeys

Homo antecessor (HOE-moe ant-ee-SESS-ur), about 780,000 years ago • Hominid found in Spain that may be the ancestor of Neandertals and possibly modern humans; many scientists do not recognize this hominid as its own species

Homo erectus (HOE-moe ee-RECT-us), about 1.8–.2 million years ago • The first hominid to leave Africa; an ancestor to later humans

Homo heidelbergensis (HOE-moe HIGH-del-bur-GEN-sis), about 800,000–200,000 years ago • Large-brained ancestor of Neandertals and modern humans; found in Europe and Africa

Homo sapiens sapiens (HOE-moe SAY-pee-ens), about 150,000 years ago–the present • Modern humans; this term means "wise, wise people"

Johanson, Donald, b. 1943 • American paleoanthropologist who discovered Lucy; director of the Institute of Human Origins in Tempe, Arizona

Kanzi (CAN-zee), b. 1980 • A bonobo, or pygmy chimp (*Pan paniscus*), born in captivity in the United States who has participated in experiments in making stone tools and learning language

Kennewick Man (KEN-uh-wick), 8,400 years ago • Skeleton of a modern human found in 1996 on the bank of the Columbia River in the state of Washington

The Kid, 25,000 years ago • The skeleton of a four-year-old child buried in a rock shelter at Lagar Velho in Portugal

Kimeu, Kamoya (KIM-yew, KAM-oy-eh), b. 1938 • Kenyan fossil hunter, famous for finding many early hominids; leader of the hominid gang

Leakey, Louis, 1903–72 • African-born anthropologist who spent much of his life searching for evidence to unravel the mystery of human origins. He excavated extensively in East Africa, particularly Olduvai Gorge

Leakey, Mary, 1913–96 • English archaeologist who uncovered the early hominid footprints at Laetoli and meticulously excavated Olduvai Gorge in Tanzania

Leakey, Meave, b. 1942 • Paleontologist who has described numerous East African fossils; wife of Richard Leakey

Leakey, **Richard**, b. 1944 • Second son of Louis and Mary Leakey; Richard, a Kenyan, has organized many paleoanthropological expeditions in Kenya

Lucy, 3.2 million years ago • A partial skeleton of a female *Australopithecus afarensis* discovered at Hadar in Ethiopia

Mellaart, **James**, b. 1925 • British archaeologist who discovered Çatalhöyük

Neandertal (nee-AND-ur-tahl), about 200,000–29,000 years ago • Close relative of modern humans, adapted to cold climates, found in Ice-Age Europe and western Asia

Orrorin tugenensis (oar-ROAR-in TOO-gen-en-sis), 6 million years ago • A candidate for the earliest hominid, but so far only fragments of fossils have been found in the Tugen Hills of Kenya

Ötzi the Iceman (OOT-see), 5,300 years ago • A well-preserved corpse of a man shot in the back with a bow and arrow

Parfitt, **Simon**, b. 1964 • A British archaeologist in charge of examining the animal bones from the site of Boxgrove, England

Roberts, **Mark**, b. 1961 • English archaeologist; director of the excavations at Boxgrove

Savage-Rumbaugh, **Sue** (SAV-ij-RUM-baw), b. 1946 • Professor of biology at Georgia State University who studies the intelligence of primates

Solecki, **Ralph** (sol-ECK-ee), b. 1917 • Directed excavations at Shanidar Cave in Iraq

Stringer, **Christopher**, b. 1948 • Paleoanthropologist at the Natural History Museum in London who argues that modern humans evolved in Africa

Tattersall, **Ian**, b. 1945 • Anthropologist at the American Museum of Natural History and author of many books on human evolution

Thorne, **Alan**, Active since 1965 • Australian paleoanthropologist who studies the first Australians

Toth, **Nicholas**, Active since 1980 • American archaeologist and stone tool–making expert

Toumai (too-MY), "Hope of Life," 7–6 million years ago • Fossil skull found in Chad that may belong to an early hominid

Turkana Boy (tur-KAHN-a), 1.6 million years ago • Almost-complete skeleton of eight-year-old *Homo erectus* boy found in Kenya by Kamoya Kimeu

Walker, **Alan**, b. 1938 • British-born anatomist and paleoanthropologist who has examined many hominids found in East Africa

White, **Tim**, b. 1950 • Professor at the University of California, Berkeley; found and described many very important hominid fossils

WoldeGabriel, **Giday** (WAHL-duh gab-ree-EL, gi-DAY), b. 1955 • Ethiopian geologist who works with Yohannes Haile-Selassie, Tim White, and others in the Afar Triangle region of Ethiopia

THE EARLY HUMAN WORLD

CANADA

NORTH AMERICA

EUROPE

RUSSIA

×Sunghir

ENGLAND
Stonehenge×
Amesbury
×Boxgrove

×Neander Valley
GERMANY
CZECH REP.
×Dolní Věstonice

Head-
Smashed-In×

×Ozette

×Knife River

×Koster

Cahokia×

×Meadowcroft
Rock Shelter

UNITED STATES

×La Brea
Tar Pits

×Clovis

×Hinds Cave

MEXICO

×Guilá Naquitz Cave

FRANCE

SPAIN
×Gran Dolina
×Lapedo Valley

PORTUGAL

×Ötzal Alps
×Chauvet Cave

ITALY

Black
Sea
REP. OF
GEORGIA
TURKEY
Catalhöyük×

Mediterranean Sea

×Dmanisi

×Abu Hureyra
SYRIA ×Shanidar Cave
IRAQ

Fertile Crescent

Sahara Desert

Nile River

AFRICA

Atlantic Ocean

Middle Awash
Valley
×

ETHIOPIA

Turkana
×

KENYA

PERU

SOUTH AMERICA

Pacific Ocean

×Olduvai Gorge
Laetoli

TANZANIA

×Swartkrans Cave

SOUTH
AFRICA

×Rapa Nui
(Easter Island)

×Klasies River Mouth

CHILE

Monte ×
Verde

SOME PRONUNCIATIONS

Abu Hureyra (A-boo hoo-RAIR-a)

Flores (FLOOR-ays)

Çatalhöyük (CHAH-tahl-HOO-yook)

Chauvet Cave (show-VAY)

Dmanisi (duh-man-EE-see)

Dolní Věstonice (DAHL-nee VEYE-es-toh-NEET-see)

Flores (FLOOR-ays)

Gran Dolina (gran dahl-EE-nah)

Guilá Naquitz (ghee-LA na-KEETZ)

Klasies River Mouth (CLAR-sees)

La Brea Tar Pits (la BRAY-ah)

Laetoli (lie-a-TOE-lee)

Lapedo Valley (la-PAY-doe)

Monte Verde (MON-tay VER-day)

Olduvai Gorge (OHL-duh-way)

Ötzal Alps (OOTS-al)

Rapa Nui (RA-pa NEW-ee)

Sunghir (SOON-gear)

Swartkrans (SWART-krans)

Zhoukoudian (jo-ko-DYEN)

CHAPTER 1

THE COSMIC JOURNEY
OUR PLACE IN TIME

Buckle up; it's going to be a bumpy ride. The car makers have built us a very special ATV. It's not only an all-terrain vehicle; it's an all-time vehicle. You're probably going to want to ride shotgun—the views are spectacular!

We begin at the beginning—literally the beginning—nearly 14 billion years ago. The headlights are on because it's pitch black. In the beams you can see the dust swirling. The dust spins faster and faster. Up ahead it's collecting into what looks like a giant CD—a CD with a smoldering fireball in the middle.

The fireball gradually changes from tomato red to white. It flashes, like a match being lit. Then it dies out. The

Pillars of gas give rise to stars such as our own sun. The Hubble telescope, which orbits the earth, took this photo of deep space with four cameras. One camera magnifies the image to show scientists more detail. When that photo is shrunk to fit the scale of the other three, the final image has a step shape.

fireball flashes again. Then it dies out again. Suddenly there is a burst of white light. We can turn off the headlights now. The sun will take over. Our time-o-meter says we're 5 billion years from home.

We're in the middle of rush-hour traffic. There are a million worlds of all sizes circling our sun. A few thousand of them are pretty big. Not a one is going to be awarded good driver of the year. A head-on collision blows two worlds to smithereens. We dodge the fragments flying past. It's cosmic bumper cars! Worlds are crashing into one another—some destroyed, others nudging one another until they crush together. All this wreckage is thinning out the traffic.

The larger worlds look as though they are crumpling. Their gravity is sucking in the bumps, smoothing the surface and creating spheres. Anything that managed to avoid a major accident is growing bigger and bigger. Now as these giants travel the beltway around the sun they pull smaller worlds into them—joining, crumpling, joining, crumpling—again and again. The smaller worlds that don't get pulled in far enough to make contact careen off course. Many are totaled in collisions. Others are yanked in by the sun and disappear in a giant fireball. More are tossed out of the galaxy into the cold. There are a few left that have found good commuter lanes. Earth is one of the lucky ones that hasn't been used as a spare part, blown up, burned up, or taken an exit ramp.

The light dims when we zoom in closer to Earth. There's still a lot of dust and gas around us. The sun's light just can't make it through. When we flick on our high beams we see a lumpy, pockmarked Earth. We watch Earth smash into smaller worlds, turning them into powder. It collects their dust like bugs on a windshield. We need our fog lights because Earth is covered in steam. The heat from all the collisions gets trapped by the vapor. Turn up the air conditioning, because things are getting hot. Earth's surface melts into an ocean of lava. It glows red.

Look out! Earth is on collision course with a big world. At first it looks as if Earth will crack in half when they crash. If the colliding world had been any bigger Earth

---

AGES OF LIFE ON EARTH

545–251 million years ago
Paleozoic Era
paleo + zoic =
"ancient" + "life"

251–65 million years ago
Mesozoic Era
meso + zoic =
"middle" + "life"

65 million years ago to the present
Cenozoic Era
ceno + zoic =
"modern" + "life"

❝ Earth's moon, 4.5 billion years after its formation

would have been blown to bits. Instead, a good-size chunk of Earth breaks off and is sent hurtling away. It's our moon.

Days on Earth are short. They're just a few hours long. Earth spins madly. But the moon begins to tug at Earth creating a drag. The moon pulls and Earth gradually slows its rotation and the days grow longer. The moon drifts off.

Below us Earth looks like it's cooling. A thin crust forms. Boiling rock spits upward from cracks in the crust. It's a volcanic fireworks display. Asteroids striking Earth raise clouds of dust—poof, poof. It's impossible to see ahead. Even the sun can't get through the mess. Turn on the heater; it's getting cold out there without the sunshine. Earth freezes. But look! There are fewer and fewer collisions now and it looks as if the dust is settling. It's a sunrise!

Turn on the windshield wipers because here comes the rain. The craters from the collisions are filling up. If we were to pull back they would look like puddles, but they are the oceans. It rains in torrents. Earth looks like a giant swimming pool. The only land we see now comes from the occasional crater rim tall enough to stick out of the water.

Splash! Splash! Comets and asteroids smash into Earth. Space dust carries life-building atoms and chemicals, jump-starting life on earth. When our time-o-meter reads 3.6 billion years from home, life has begun to blossom.

We're cruising along at about 3 billion years from home when land starts forming on Earth. But, look—the continents are moving all around in slow motion. They're crashing into one another. On impact they buckle like a front fender in a car wreck. The crust crinkles and mountain ranges thrust upward. Volcanoes erupt. Lava leaks.

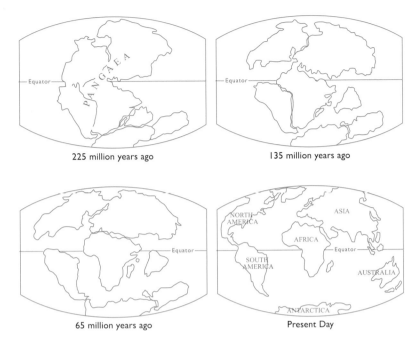

225 million years ago

135 million years ago

65 million years ago

Present Day

Think of the earth as a hard-boiled egg. Both the egg and the earth have three main layers. Crack the shell of the egg and slide the pieces around on the slippery white. This is how the tectonic plates move across the earth's mantle. The yolk represents the earth's core.

Earth's thin crust is not an unbroken coating like the shell of an egg. It is made up of a dozen or more giant drifting plates. The continents ride these floating solid rock slabs called tectonic plates.

Now the time-o-meter reads 600 million years from home. Earth looks nothing like the globe we live on. There's no land at all on the northern half. It's all water. One giant clump of land sits in the southern half. The land moves. It's moving at the same speed it will always move—about an inch a year. A tree grows faster than that. But since we're whizzing through time the land looks as though it is zipping around the globe. One minute there are two chunks of land, the next there is one huge supercontinent. Earth looks like a water planet with one island.

It's getting hot again. Let's hope the snails don't mind the heat. Wait; is that a bug coming out of the ocean?

There's no slowing down now. We're 255 million years from home and we're dodging plumes of molten lava shooting into the sky. Hold on, there's lots of turbulence. That island on Earth is beginning to break up. Things are getting rocky. Rain is pelting us. Volcanoes are erupting. Landmasses

Snail fossil, Iowa, United States, 300 million years ago

are smashing into landmasses. The reptiles don't even seem to notice.

When our time-o-meter hits the 100-million-year mark, South America and Africa split. They are forced apart by movement below them. You can see where they used to fit together; now a river of ocean separates them. Why that's a horseshoe crab! Things are starting to look more familiar—but not quite. There are oceans inside the continents. And through it all, the dinosaur walks.

Watch out! Incoming asteroid. Direct hit with Earth. What's that stink like rotten eggs? Sulfur! Sulfur and dust. The asteroid knocks it all into the air. We're 65 million years from home. The dust is blocking out the sun. The dinosaurs are dying.

From where we're watching we can see the continents drifting farther apart. India collides with Asia and mountains crumple upward. Is that a monkey? It looks a bit like

66 Horseshoe crab fossil, Eichstatt, Germany, 150 million years ago

Monkey-like primates feast on fruits in this artist's reconstruction from fossil evidence. About 34 million years ago, the part of Egypt in this painting was a lush rainforest, not the desert it is today.

one. The trees are full of them. Life is changing so quickly now it's a blur.

To give us an idea of how rapidly life on Earth progressed in the scheme of this 14-billion-year cosmic journey, imagine squeezing all the events into a single calendar year. We begin time on New Year's Day and end in the present, when the clock strikes midnight one year later. It would be September on our "all-time calendar" before our solar system took shape. A week later Earth would form. Two weeks after that life appears on Earth. In early October our oldest rocks crop up out of that global ocean.

In December, Earth is beefing up its atmosphere with oxygen. Now things begin to happen fast:

December 20—we see the first fish in those oceans.

December 21—Earth loses that barren rock look when plants begin to grow on land.

December 22—insects and animals follow the plants.

December 23—the first trees, the first reptiles.

December 26—the dinosaurs!

December 29—the first birds.

December 30—dinosaurs become extinct just as the first flowers bloom.

The last day of the year dawns and humans are still nowhere in sight. The day drags on as we look for evidence of others like us. It's 8:10 in the evening before the first **hominids** appear. We're hominids, but these fellows don't look much like us at all. They look more like our ape cousins walking around on two legs. With only eight minutes left until the clock strikes twelve there are *still* no humans.

Almost everything we know about humans from written history happens in that last ten-second countdown—10, 9, 8, 7. . . . To discover our unwritten past—what happened in those moments before the countdown—we need to turn our all-time vehicle back into an all-terrain vehicle. We're going to drive straight down inside Earth. We're going to plunge into the crust. It's a graveyard down there. It's time to dig up the past.

A hominid is a member of the family of mammals named *Hominidae*. We humans, big-brained hominids with articulate speech, are the only surviving species of this family. Extinct hominids include all the species discussed in this book that habitually walked on two legs.

CHAPTER 2

THE BIG DIG
THE EARLIEST HOMINIDS—
SO FAR

A lion roared in the distance. It would be dawn soon. Yohannes Haile-Selassie pulled the sleeping bag over his shoulder, wishing for a few more minutes of sleep. He would soon go out again into the Ethiopian scrubland. Maybe today would be the day—the day he would find hominid bones. "When you don't find anything, an hour is like a day. But when you find good stuff, you don't even want night to come, you want to work 24 hours to find more." Maybe today would be that kind of day—a day when he wouldn't want night to come.

Haile-Selassie wore a baseball cap to shield his eyes from the sun. He and his partner Giday WoldeGabriel stared out across the stony, sunbaked ground. Was this a good spot for

SKULLDUGGERY

We commonly talk about "bones" when there is no bone left at all. An archaeological find may look like a bone, but the bone has been replaced by minerals and now is a fossil. People also commonly use the words "skull" and "cranium" interchangeably. But a skull is actually a cranium and a jaw-bone. When the jaw-bone is missing, as it often is, technically you have just a cranium.

SCIENCES THAT STUDY THE PAST		
Anthropology	*anthropo* + *ology* = "man" + "study"	the study of humans
Geology	*geo* + *ology* = "earth" + "study"	the study of rocks and Earth's history
Paleoecology	*paleo* + *eco* + *ology* = "ancient" + "environment" + "study"	the study of ancient environments
Paleontology	*paleo* + *onto* + *ology* = "ancient" + "existing" + "study"	the study of life on Earth in ancient times through fossils
Paleo-anthropology	*paleo* + *anthropo* + *ology* = "ancient" + "man" + "study"	the study of ancient humans

Haile-Selassie is an anthropologist. WoldeGabriel is a geologist. A dig requires the combined skills from scholars of many kinds of sciences.

Erosion from wind and rare desert rainstorms expose fossils of animals that lived in this Ethiopian desert landscape when the climate was wetter than it is today.

fossils? If something died here would it have been quickly covered and protected from scavengers? Because given a chance, scavengers will rip apart, crunch and munch, and scatter bones—and that's not good for fossil hunters. They wondered if this was once a riverbed where water tumbled along, carrying whatever fell in and jumbling the bones for miles—that's not good for fossil hunters, either.

WoldeGabriel squinted, trying to picture the landscape 6 million years ago. The boulders and pebbles scattered over the desert in front of him faded away. He didn't see the sparse scrub brush or the cracked earth. He didn't feel the temperature beginning to rise with the sun. Before him the landscape blossomed into what existed millions of years ago. He felt moist air. He saw a lush forest. He heard the rumble of volcanoes. From the pages of the *Washington Post* WoldeGabriel tells us, "in this particular area, most of the volcanoes erupted through lakes and groundwater." WoldeGabriel said, "During the eruptions, it was very hostile."

HOW TO BECOME A FOSSIL

Becoming a fossil is a matter of luck. When an animal dies, it often is torn apart by scavengers, or stepped on and crushed, or scattered by rain and wind. If it is buried quickly, its chances of turning into a fossil are better. Under the protective layer of mud, sand, or ash, the animal will rot, leaving hard parts such as teeth and bones. Slowly, what was once alive is replaced by minerals. Fossils aren't just made from animals—they can be from plants, shells, dung, or even footprints.

THE BURIED PAST

The past gets buried under layers and layers of dirt carried by wind and water, under rotting plants, under lava flows, or even under trash we throw away. One important way archaeologists date fossils is by the layer in which they are found. The deeper down you go, the farther you travel back in time. Ancient layers can be exposed by erosion, or forced to the surface by earthquakes.

It was hostile for hominids, but it was good for fossil making. Volcanic ash rains down helping to preserve what it covers. Lava flows and traps things, too. Eruptions do something else that scientists appreciate. Eruptions make it possible to pinpoint the age of a fossil. Volcanic rock contains radioactive material, and radioactive material can be dated. They can learn just how old the fossils were—and that *is* good for fossil hunters.

The two Ethiopian scholars decided where the day's work should begin. The place they chose "was very steep and very rugged, with most of the surfaces covered by loose rock," said WoldeGabriel. "The [layers] we were looking for just poked through the surface." This was a promising place.

Armed with trowels, they began to carefully move dirt and small pebbles into pails. Workers carried the full pails away and replaced them with empty pails. They moved in slow motion, struggling against the heat. Haile-Selassie tied a bandana around his neck. Sand and grit mixed with his sweat and collected in the folds of his skin. He stood and stretched his cramped legs. He drank from his canteen, wiping his mouth with the back of his hand.

Off to the side, two students on either end of a screen framed in wood pushed and pulled, sifting the sand that the workers had lugged over in the pails. Sand and dirt fell in clouds, leaving bits too large to fit through the holes bouncing over the screen bed. Haile-Selassie watched as they sorted through the bits, picking bone fragments from among the pebbles. Each identified bone added another detail to the picture. What did they learn from that small chunk of a monkey skull? There must have been trees—a forest, in fact. And what did that antelope horn reveal? That particular antelope favored a wild grass that must have grown here. Like a jigsaw puzzle slowly pieced together, little by little a picture from 6 million years ago of this place called the Middle Awash was filling in.

Haile-Selassie stared off, looking at the scattered pebbles. Suddenly a pattern in the rocks became visible. It seemed to stand out from the random placement of light stones. Without taking his eyes from the spot he hooked his finger around the string tied at his neck and fished out his hand lens. He crouched over the rim of fossil barely above the ground.

With a dental pick he carefully scraped dirt away from a single tooth and from the surface of a jawbone, reaching now and then for his paintbrush to brush away the loose sand. The thrill he felt chilled him. A perfect arc of jawbone emerged from the sun-baked desert floor.

The workers and his friends came one by one until they surrounded Haile-Selassie. Later, *National Geographic* magazine recounted Haile-Selassie's speculations about the jawbone's origins. "It could be the earliest hominid, or it could be a common ancestor, or it gave rise only to the chimpanzee lineage, or it went extinct around 6 million years ago without giving rise to any species."

Haile-Selassie found more fossils from what he believes to be at least five individuals. He named this hominid *Ardipithecus ramidus kadabba,* which means root-ape ancestor. Was this the root of humankind? What could he learn from this Root-ape, who was about the size of a modern chimpanzee? What could he learn from the fossils? From the angle of the toe bone, Haile-Selassie learned that when Root-ape walked he left the front part of his foot on the ground and lifted his heel—like we do. Apes walk on the outside of their feet. From the wear on the teeth, he learned that Root-ape ate leaves and fruit. The fossils are painting the portrait of our ancestor. It's not a likeness of our grandfather, or of our great-grandfather, or even of our great-great-grandfather, but of an ancestor from 300,000 generations ago.

The picture of human evolution is drawn with the fossils that scientists such as Haile-Selassie and WoldeGabriel dig up.

Many scientists thought that hominids had split from the apes because of climate changes 5 million years ago. Drier weather was turning forests into grasslands. They thought

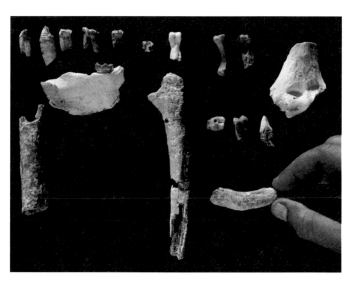

" *Ardipithecus ramidus kadabba* bones and teeth, Middle Awash Valley, Ethiopia, 6 million years ago

" *Ardipithecus ramidus kadabba* tooth, Middle Awash Valley, Ethiopia, 6 million years ago

EARLIEST HOMINID?

No one argues about how old Toumai is, or whether or not it was an important find, but the claim that it is "hominid" is in hot debate. One group of scientists is convinced that the skull and jaw fragments come from the face of the earliest hominid discovered so far. Another group is just as sure that Toumai was an ape. Everyone wants their bundle of bones to be from the earliest hominid. Some of the loudest challenges to Toumai's lineage are from scientists who discovered *Orrorin tugenensis*—or "Millennium Man," nicknamed after the year 2000, when the bones were found. Naturally, they would like their discovery to be the earliest hominid. If it is Toumai, it can't be Millennium Man.

Is Toumai a hominid or an ape? Either way this is an important discovery. It brings us closer to the last common ancestor of ape and human. It's another puzzle piece to our past. Where it fits in the picture is yet to come.

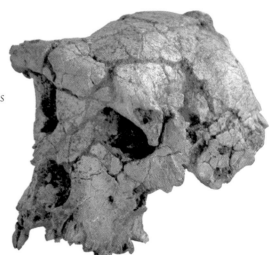

A team digging in the African desert of Chad found a skull from between 6 and 7 million years ago. The skull is called Toumai, which means "hope of life," a nickname given to children born in the dry season.

that some apes were born with something that gave them an advantage in the grasslands. They thought that whatever that difference was, it gave rise to hominids. These scientists expected to find the first hominids in the African grasslands. The *Washington Post* quotes Haile-Selassie describing what was unexpected about his find. Instead of living in the grasslands, "the creature lived along with ancient elephants, antelopes, horses, monkeys and rhinoceroses in what was then a lush mountain forest periodically destroyed by volcanic eruptions." Later, tests showed that Root-ape was almost 6 million years old, adding more evidence to the idea that the split was earlier than scientists had previously thought. "These fossils are strong evidence that lines leading to chimpanzees and humans had already split well before five million years ago," Haile-Selassie said.

"It is hard to imagine that life would go on normally under such hostile environmental conditions," WoldeGabriel said. "*Ardipithecus* and the other animals inhabiting the area were real survivors."

Night fell on the camp in the Ethiopian scrubland. Lanterns made the tent walls glow and soft voices rose and fell. A lion looked down on the camp, then huffed and turned to hunt elsewhere. The day had been a good one. Despite tired, aching muscles from hours spent stooping, sleep wouldn't come easy. Who knew what they would find tomorrow?

CHAPTER 3

WHO'S THE FAIREST OF THEM ALL?

OUR PLACE IN NATURE

❝ CHARLES DARWIN

Yeroen swaggered up to the drums and began to play rhythmically. He started with a slow beat. Luit noticed his friend at the drums and began bobbing his head in time. Nikkie ran to join them, hooting and grabbing a handful of sand to toss into the air. Krom is deaf, but she could tell from the expressions of the others that something was going on, so she hooted, too. Yeroen leaped up onto the drum and alternated between striking it with his fists and jumping on it. Big Mama sat a short distance away, leaning against a tree and shaking her head.

A common chimpanzee catches up with the news. A chimp can't read, of course, but it can admire the photos in this magazine.

Is this some sort of rock band? In a way it is. Yeroen, Luit, Nikkie, Krom, and Big Mama are part of a band of chimpanzees that live at Burgers' Zoo in Holland. By watching— a whole *lot* of watching—scientists are not only learning about chimpanzees, but they are also learning about us.

If you arrived from another planet and landed in the stands of an American football game, you wouldn't understand what was happening on the field at first. People leap on top of one another into piles, throw a ball around, kick it now and again, then stop the ferocious aggression for a group hug—all while a few puny men in stripes run around the edges blowing whistles. If you watched long enough, eventually things would begin to make sense. You would start to understand the rules of the game because the behavior would repeat often enough to reveal some logical explanation. During that hug people looked like they were planning something. One guy always seemed to get the ball first. The ball must be a valuable thing because everyone fights for it, but they have very short memories because they quickly forget about it and walk away.

All right, so maybe you didn't get everything right. But some of your deductions were correct. The longer you watched, the more you would understand. Scientists watching the chimpanzees at Burgers' Zoo are beginning to understand some things. They are understanding more and more about chimpanzees' social life and are finding they are more like humans than we ever imagined.

Until fairly recently, humans didn't want to think that we were related to animals. We considered ourselves above animals. Even the scientific name for humans is pretty conceited—*Homo sapiens* means "the wise person." No one believed that animals could be that smart. People believed that animals behaved the way they did because of instinct. Animals couldn't feel anger or happiness or

Charles Darwin was 42 when he sat for this photograph. Darwin might never have published his books on evolution if other scientists hadn't pushed him. He did not like confrontation and knew his theories would spark bitter debate, which they still do today, more than 100 years later.

even pain. It would be interesting to introduce these people to Jimmie, a chimpanzee at Burgers' Zoo. Like all chimpanzees, Jimmie likes to play games. She pokes a straw between the bars at passing humans. She holds it out to them. A present—for you—she offers sweetly. When someone reaches for it, Jimmie's other hand flashes out and nabs the poor sucker's arm. It takes several zookeepers to pry Jimmie off the unsuspecting human. She loves this trick and plays it over and over. Not so stupid after all.

One of the first people to understand our relationship to animals was the English naturalist Charles Darwin. In the 19th century most people believed all life had been created at once, just as we see it today, and that nothing had changed ever since. Darwin's theory was the complete opposite. He believed all life sprang from a common origin and was still changing. He wrote in his book *The Descent of Man*, "Man is descended from a hairy. . . **quadruped**." Most people misunderstood what Darwin was trying to say. They thought he was telling them that humans had descended from modern apes. This started a wild goose chase that would go on for a century—the search for the "missing link," the link between ape and human. What Darwin was trying to say was *not* that apes and humans were in the same line, like two connecting links in a chain, but that they both split off from a common apelike ancestor long, long ago. We are cousins, not grandparent and grandchild.

Darwin would not have been surprised at all to see the chimpanzees at Burgers' Zoo make their great escape. Rock, one of the oldest in the group, found the perfect branch. With some help from the others, he leaned it up against an outside wall. They climbed over the top, using the branch for a ladder, Rock in the lead. Hours later, Big Mama was found in a local restaurant, perched on the counter by the cash register sipping from a bottle of chocolate milk. Their enclosure is now patrolled daily for dead branches lying about. But don't worry, the chimpanzees have figured out how to use keys and are quite good at picking the zookeeper's pockets. They'll get out again. It's only a matter of time— and planning.

HAPPY BIRTHDAY

Charles Darwin and Abraham Lincoln were born on the same day, February 12, 1809.

{ *quadru* + *ped* = "four" + "foot" If you walk on all four feet, you're a quadruped.

Charles Darwin, *The Descent of Man,* 1871

A young chimpanzee uses a thin stick to fish in a log for termites or ants to eat. Chimps also use other tools, such as stones, to crack open nuts.

Darwin argued that apes could reason, use tools, imitate, and remember—all qualities that most people at the time thought only humans possessed. Rock certainly used reason to plan his escape, and, in the wild, chimpanzees make tools. They strip leaves off twigs, so the long narrow sticks can fit into termite tunnels. They poke the stick into termite nests, then pull it out and eat the termites clinging to the stick.

Imitate? At Burgers' Zoo, Krom may have something to say about that. "Krom" means crooked in Dutch. She got her name because she stands hunched over. Chimpanzees are always inventing new games, and for a while the hot new game at the zoo was to follow Krom, single file, mimicking her crooked walk. Krom couldn't hear what was going on behind her, which probably was a good thing. The others thought that this was hilarious.

Many 19th-century scientists believed in the gradual change that Darwin called evolution. They could see how changes came about. If an animal was born with something that, by chance, gave it an edge—an advantage over the others—it had a better chance at survival. It would live to pass that advantage down to its children, and they would pass it down to theirs. Soon those with the edge outnumbered those without it. Darwin called this process natural selection.

But even Darwin's followers thought he had gone a step too far in his book *The Expression of Emotions in Man and Animals*. In it Darwin claimed we share our emotions with many species—our fear, our grief, our joy, and our loyalty. We reveal the connection in the way we express our emotions. "The anthropoid apes . . . utter a . . . sound, corresponding with our laughter, when they are tickled, especially under the armpits."

In the Burgers' Zoo, a chimpanzee named Gorilla (how confusing—a chimpanzee named Gorilla!) had several babies over the years. They all died even though she was a tender, loving mother. Each time an infant died, she would grieve for weeks, huddled in a corner, ignoring the others, breaking out into screams now and again. Chimpanzees feel deeply. Do you think Darwin went too far?

Chimpanzees are our closest living relatives. They can catch our diseases. They can give us blood. They have unique fingerprints like we do. They can even speak to us. Jane Goodall, who has spent her life watching chimpanzees in the wild, wrote in her book *Chimps,* "They taught the sign language that deaf people use to a young chimp named Washoe. She learned over 300 signs. She even invented signs of her own. She called a fizzing soda a 'listen drink,' a piece of celery 'pipe food,' a duck on a pond 'water bird.'"

Humans and chimpanzees can recognize themselves in a mirror. They are aware of themselves. If you put a mirror in front of most animals, they will behave as if another animal has just entered the room. They'll growl, attack, play, sniff—until they get bored and walk away. The professor of primate behavior Frans de Waal wrote about the chimpanzees at Burgers' Zoo in his book *Peacemaking among Primates,* "Apes . . . start using the looking glass to inspect body parts (teeth, buttocks) that they normally cannot see. They also amuse themselves by making strange faces at their reflection, or by decorating themselves (placing vegetables on their heads, for instance)." Nobody said that just because you were self-aware, you were guaranteed fashion sense.

With so many similarities, you may be wondering how humans and apes are different. After all, we *are* different.

66 Charles Darwin, *The Expressions of Emotions of Man and Animals, 1873*

CHARMED BY CHIMPS

From the time Jane Goodall was a little girl reading Dr. Doolittle, she knew she would one day end up in the African forest among the wild animals. When she first arrived in Africa she worked in Kenya with the anthropologist Louis Leakey. He encouraged her to follow her passion and observe chimpanzees in the wild—observations he believed would answer questions to our own beginnings.

We're not as hairy, for one thing. Our faces are flatter. We walk on two feet instead of four, and our brains, although similar, are bigger.

We see so much of ourselves in Yeroen's expressive face that it is tempting to jump to false conclusions. It is tempting to believe that he is our primitive self—that we evolved from the apes—that Yeroen looks just like we would have millions of years ago. But that's not true. Yeroen has come as far in time from his primitive ancestor as we have come from ours. Both of us are long removed from the common ancestor we once shared.

The evolutionary process doesn't behave like a vine, groping higher and higher. It behaves more like a bush, branching off in all directions, each twig stretching outward

An infant chimp named Hoya holds out her hand to Mama asking for a hug or a kiss. Mama was 37 years old when this photo was taken.

CHIMPS AND HUMANS, BY THE BOOK		
	Chimpanzee	**Human**
Superfamily	*Hominoidea*	*Hominoidea*
Family	*Pongidae* (Great Apes)	*Hominidae*
Genus	*Pan*	*Homo*
Species	*troglodytes* (common chimp)	*sapiens*

on its own. Many of the twigs come to dead ends, representing extinct species. Some continue to divide as new species branch off from their parents. The twig that represents Yeroen split from the twig that represents us a few million years ago.

Look around. Imagine every living thing, past and present, represented by a tip of a twig on that giant evolutionary bush. Imagine millions of species represented by millions of twig ends. The evolutionary bush is pretty unwieldy. Making sense out of it and all the organisms it symbolizes would be impossible without a system. In order to distinguish where we fit and where the chimps fit—where *any* living thing fits—in the animal and plant kingdoms, scientists have created a system that groups things according to their similarities and their differences. **Taxonomy** is the science that wrestles with the challenge of grouping living things according to their relationships to one another. The names of the groups are in Latin so that scientists all over the world can understand them.

Back at Burgers' Zoo there's a happy ending in the making. Gorilla, the chimpanzee whose babies died, has been given a foster child. Every afternoon Gorilla must take her new baby inside to feed her a bottle while the others stay outside. When the keeper calls to Gorilla to let her know it's time to go inside with her baby, Gorilla goes first to Yeroen and then to Big Mama, pats them, and kisses them good-bye.

taxis + *onomy* = "arrangement" + "many names"
The classification of all living things is certainly an arrangement of many names.

CHAPTER 4

A WALK ON THE WILD SIDE
BIPEDS STEP OUT

Louis and Mary Leakey, who were husband and wife, often worked together in Africa. Midday, when the heat is at its worst, is a good time to clean, catalog, and catch up on paperwork.

One afternoon in September 1976, the archaeologist Mary Leakey was busy cataloging the fossils and artifacts spread across her worktable. She loved feeling the weight of the pieces in her hand—holding things that someone else had held millions of years before. It gave her a strange sensation to know that someone like her, but not like her, may once have turned it over just as she was doing now. She picked up a fossilized leaf that looked like a present-day acacia leaf and made notes in her field book. Her dog, Sophie, flopped down by her feet. Sophie alternated between panting and licking her forepaw that had been cut by a wild asparagus thorn. Leakey noticed her guests starting out for an afternoon walk. She may have warned them to watch out for the poisonous puff adders. Pay attention to the starlings, she would have said, the birds will squawk if a snake is nearby.

The heat of the African day had cooled pleasantly when the visiting scholars set out across the paleontological site, Laetoli in the Serengeti Plain of northern Tanzania. Serengeti comes from a word the local people, the Maasai, use meaning "endless plains." And indeed, the open grasslands seemed to reach to the horizon. The scholars followed the dried-up riverbed. Now and then they passed a muddy puddle that stank of rhino urine. They probably swapped complaints about the jaw-rattling ride to the site. There were no roads to Laetoli and the grass was tall. Vehicles overheated again and again when grass seed clogged the radiators.

Elephants had passed through a riverbed days before. Bowling-ball-sized clumps of

sunbaked elephant dung clotted the path. The temptation was too much for these distinguished scholars. Within seconds dung was zooming in all directions. One scholar ducked, avoiding a ball of dung bigger than his head. He scooped a handful and wound up to throw, but his feet must have tangled when he turned, and he fell. Holding one hand up, fingers spread as wide as possible to protect his head, face turned to the ground, he must have begged for mercy. Then his cries changed from pleading to disbelief. Quick, he would have urged his colleagues, come look.

His friends stepped forward carefully, possibly wondering if this was just a trick to get them within firing range. But instantly they were all down on their knees. All thoughts of elephant dung were forgotten. Hundreds of fossilized animal tracks were locked in the rock-hard, compacted volcanic ash known as tuff.

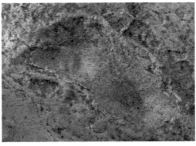

 Fossilized footprint, Laetoli, Tanzania, 3.6 million years ago

Mary Leakey wrote about Laetoli in her autobiography, *Disclosing the Past,* "Of all my major projects, Laetoli was certainly one of the most demanding, . . . but it also proved one of the most worthwhile." Although Laetoli was loaded with fossils, scientists were most excited about the dramatic area known as Footprint Tuff. Mary Leakey explained why it is so important: "There are a number of sites in the world that have produced animal tracks, though none in such extraordinary quantities and variety as Laetoli." And they *are* varied. She wrote, "literally tens of thousands of prints have been found in this deposit, ranging from the trail left by an insect, and the tracks of birds, to the footprints of large elephants."

As exciting as it was to uncover prints made by animals such as a three-toed horse, it was nothing compared to what they found two years later. Captured in the volcanic tuff was evidence that more than 3.5 million years ago, three hominids decided to take a stroll—walking upright and on two legs.

What made these footprints last? A nearby volcano helped preserve them. The six-inch-thick Footprint Tuff is made up of layers—a layer for each volcanic eruption. Each eruption shot a cloud of fine ash up into the sky. The ash fell onto the ground like beach sand. Then rain fell softly, soaking the ash until it turned to mud. Animals slogged through the mud, leaving depressions that hardened when the sun baked the ash. It dried like cement. And then the volcano erupted again and more animals walked through. This sequence repeated at least six times until one massive volcanic flare-up sealed the whole lot of tracks in a thick layer of ash. Gradually, over millions of years, water and wind wore through until one day three scholars—dodging dung—fell on them.

bi + peds = "two" + "feet"
If you walk on two feet,
you're a biped.

Walking on two legs is one of the things that makes us human. There are other mammals that are **bipeds**—kangaroos, for example. But kangaroos hop. A hop is nothing like our heel-toe stride. Monkeys and apes can walk on two legs for short periods of time, but they quickly get tired. Humans have a long spine that curves, allowing them to center their weight over their lower body for balance. Apes have to stand with their feet wide apart forcing them to throw their weight from side to side when they walk. And because they can't lock their knee joints to stand on a straight leg, their muscles must work to hold them upright.

This trail of footprints in Laetoli, Tanzania, is proof that hominids walked upright 3.6 million years ago.

Mary Leakey wrote about evenings with her friends at the Laetoli dig, "I found myself sitting at the head of a longer table than I could remember on any dig, with the line of faces on each side seeming to stretch away into the darkness." It was a good time to wonder and to share ideas. There is one question that was certain to have come up—*Why would animals that had always scurried through the treetops come down to the ground and walk on two feet?* The scholars spent more than one evening talking about possible explanations for why our ancestors stood up:

Did our earliest ancestor stand up to hunt dinner? Some scholar would have pointed out there was no evidence of hunting at that time.

So if the earliest hominids were scavengers, did they stand up to follow herds waiting for one of the animals to die and then feast on the carcass? Some scholar must have mentioned how hard it would be to keep up with fast moving herds and that even if it were easy, hominids began standing in the forest. Forest-dwelling animals don't form herds.

Standing tall can look fierce and scare off enemies— another possibility.

What if the hominids were eating as if they were at an outdoor buffet, standing as they moved from one low bush to another low bush to a low branch? It could have begun this way *in* the trees, eating while standing on branches.

What *was* it that made us stand up on two feet? Imagine yourself living like our earliest ancestors millions of years ago in the forest or woodland. What would make you stand up?

WHICH CAME FIRST?

Walking on two legs is one of the main features that defines humans. Another is big brains. Scientists have argued for years which came first. Footprint Tuff settled that argument. The hominids who walked upright through the volcanic tuff had brains the size of a chimpanzee's. Hominids were bipeds before they were big-brained.

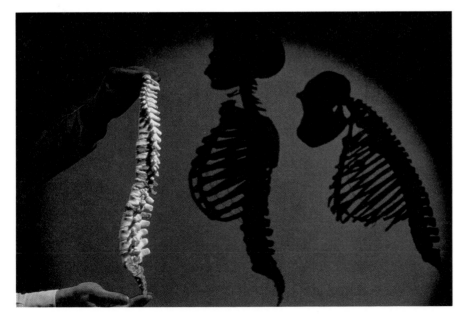

These spines come from (left to right) the hominid species that made the Laetoli footprints, a modern human, and a chimpanzee. The fact that the hominid and modern human spines are similar is evidence supporting the theory that hominids walked upright more than 3 million years ago.

CHAPTER 5

LUCY
THE FAMILY BUSH: MORE HOMINIDS

In a desert region of Ethiopia called the Afar Triangle not much grows. The monotonous gray ground stretches in all directions. Gravel and fist-sized rocks roll underfoot. They crunch, crunch, crunch with each step. It hardly ever rains, but when it does, it comes down hard and fast. With no vegetation to hold it, the surface dirt washes away. What lay hidden the day before is exposed. If it is a fossil that surfaces, and no one finds it, the next rain, or the one after, or the one after that, will wash it away. Knowing this makes the fossil hunters a bit anxious as they crunch, crunch, crunch, up and down the gullies cut from rushing rainwater. They walk a bit stooped, searching—always searching. There's a spot in the middle of the Afar desert along a muddy slow-moving river called the Awash that is

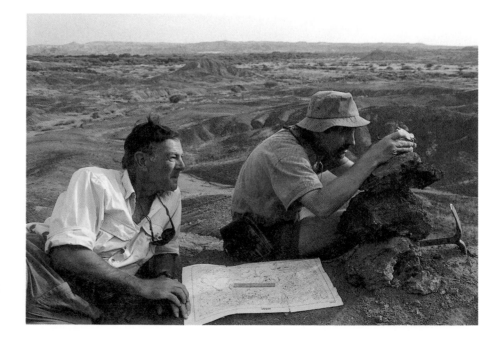

Donald Johanson (left), an anthropologist, and Bob Walter, a geologist, use a map and compass to pinpoint their position in the desert at Hadar, Ethiopia.

a favorite of the anthropologist Donald Johanson. If ever there were a case for "right time, right place," this is it. The time was November 30, 1974. The place was Hadar.

Donald Johanson woke to the smell of fresh coffee perking. He could hear the Afar tribesmen who worked for the expedition tending their goats and camels. The day had begun.

Tom Gray joined his teacher, Johanson, for coffee. Gray had come to Hadar to study plant and animal fossils. He was piecing together a picture of ancient climates from life millions of years ago. Gray had hoped to get a look at Locality 162, but wasn't sure where that particular site was among the hundreds on the master map. Johanson was behind on his homework and hesitated, but something—something stemming from that fossil hunter's anxiety—urged him to take Gray out to Locality 162.

They parked their vehicle on the slope of a gully and for the next several hours Johanson and Gray walked a methodical grid—back and forth—coming at the same place from different angles—scanning the ground—back and forth—back and forth—searching. The desert temperature rose to 110 degrees—back and forth they crunched. They'd found bits and pieces—some antelope teeth, a chunk of a monkey's jaw, the skull of an extinct horse. The heat had finally worn them out and they decided to head back to their vehicle. Johanson writes in *Lucy: The Beginnings of Humankind* that he suggested, "Let's go back this way and survey the bottom of that little gully over there."

Once in the gully they realized there was nothing of much interest. Hot, tired, and hungry, they started up the slope. Partway up Johanson noticed a bone. With a calm he was not feeling he said, "That's a bit of a hominid arm." When they bent to examine it, Johanson spotted the back of a skull, then a leg bone, then a backbone, then a pelvis. . . . Johanson writes, "An unbelievable . . . thought flickered through my mind. Suppose all

HADAR

Hadar is an area of about 50 square miles in the Awash Valley of northeastern Ethiopia. Many fossils in Hadar are eroding out of sediments that are between about 4 and 2.5 million years old.

❝ Horse jaw, Middle Awash Valley, Ethiopia, 3.2 million years ago

This fossilized jaw of a horse was discovered at Hadar. The enamel on the teeth, glinting in the sunlight, is not worn down because this horse died when it was still young.

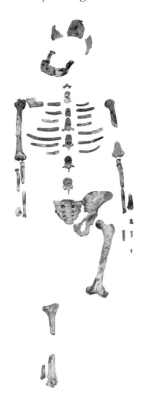

Australopithecus afarensis bones, Hadar, Ethiopia, 3.2 million years ago

these fitted together? Could they be parts of a single, extremely primitive skeleton? No such skeleton had ever been found—anywhere."

They found bone after hominid bone. The two men jumped up and down, hugging and shouting, "I can't believe it! I can't believe it!" The crunch, crunch, crunch underfoot stopped them both. There were pieces of skeleton all around them. Before they damaged something, they marked the spot and returned to camp, skidding in and honking the horn wildly.

For three weeks every scientist and tribesman in camp worked that gully—even the small children helped out. When it was all over they had recovered hundreds of bones—some barely bits. There were no duplicates. Sometimes you find a piece of a right arm, then a piece of another right arm. Not in this gully. The bones came from one individual. Johanson and his team had nearly 40 percent of the skeleton—40 percent of something that had lived 3.18 million years ago. It was incredible that so much of it had stayed together that long. Once the fossils surfaced, it was only a matter of a few rainstorms before the fossils would have been swept away, jumbled and lost. No wonder anthropologists are anxious.

That night at camp it was party time. Everyone was too excited to sleep. Someone put on a Beatles tape and blasted "Lucy in the Sky with Diamonds" over and over and over. Johanson doesn't remember exactly when during the night it happened, or who started it, but suddenly everyone was calling the skeleton Lucy. And as nicknames often do, it stuck. She has a lovely Ethiopian name, Dinquinesh, which means "thou art wonderful," and wonderful she is, but to the world she would soon be known as Lucy.

Lucy didn't look much like a human being. For one thing, she was small. She was a full-grown adult, but stood only about three and a half feet tall, and her head wasn't much bigger than a softball. Johanson writes in *Lucy*, "On the hominid line the earliest ones are too primitive to be called humans. They must be given another name. Lucy is in that category." What *would* Johanson call her?

The next field season Johanson got lucky again. This time he found not one individual, but what he described as a "cascade of bones," so many that they appeared to be pouring from the hillside. Remains of at least 13 individuals were scattered down the slope. The skeletons were like Lucy, but bigger—males, females, infants, and juveniles—the First Family. It appeared as if the entire group had died together. Had a flash flood trapped them? This was just one of many questions Johanson would lose sleep over.

He kept returning to the dilemma of what to call Lucy—and now the question became what to call "them." They would have to have a scientific name. Scientists the world over use Latin names to classify members of the plant and animal kingdom. What would they call Lucy? Lucy was a hominid, so it was clear to Johanson that she belonged in the same family as humans, *Hominidae*. But what about her genus? Her species? Was she *Homo*—a member of our own genus? Or was she *Australopithecus*—our hominid cousin? There was only one way to answer that question, and the work involved would take years to accomplish. Each of the hundreds of fossils had to be carefully cleaned. Then countless measurements taken and recorded in notebook after notebook. All these tasks had to be completed before Johanson could even begin to answer the question of what place the Hadar hominids would take in our evolutionary history.

Australopithecus afarensis bones, Hadar, Ethiopia, 3.5–3 million years ago

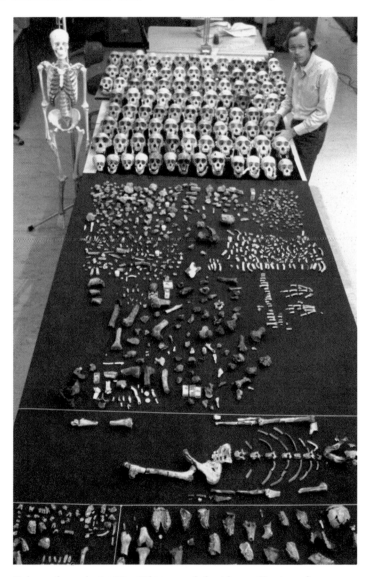

Paleoanthropologist Tim White stands beside a collection of chimpanzee skulls and the fossils of Australopithecus afarensis *discovered at Hadar and Laetoli. The fossils include Lucy, who appears as a partial skeleton near the bottom of the photo.*

"When Don showed me the first knee joint, I told him to go back and find me a whole animal. He obliged with Lucy. So I told him to go back again and get me some variety. The next year he found Mom and Pop and the kids."

—Anthropologist C. Owen Lovejoy,
***Lucy: The Beginning of Humankind*, 1981**

OUR COUSINS

Thousands of fossil hominid bones and teeth found in several African countries, as well as the hominids who made the Laetoli footprints, belong in the genus *Australopithecus*. "Australopithecus" comes from the Latin word "Australis," meaning "southern," and the Greek word "Pithekos," meaning "ape." However, this "southern ape," which was first found in South Africa, is not an ape, but a hominid.

After cleaning, organizing, and measuring, Johanson could no longer avoid addressing what Lucy's scientific name should be. He writes in *Lucy*, "Alone in my office one night in the basement of the Cleveland Museum, I got out all the jaws and lined them up on the table." Johanson recalls that in the solitude of his lab, he "stared at the jaws, at the rows of pearly gray teeth, the rough brown jawbones. Sitting there, unlabeled, unidentified, they seemed to mock me. 'What are we?' they whispered. 'We are three million years old.'. . . I had found them. Now what was I going to do with them?"

So what scientific name did Johanson finally give Lucy? She is officially known as a member of the species *Australopithecus afarensis*, named after the region where Johanson had found her—the Afar Triangle.

The Afar is a desert today, but millions of years ago it was a grassland with lakes, and, as it turns out, home to many hominids other than Lucy. Luck may play a part in finding those hominids, but as most paleoanthropologists know, it's really about hard work. Paleoanthropologist Tim White is no stranger to the physical demands in the field and the mental demands in the lab. His efforts in the Afar gave us a surprise—literally. White and his colleagues found several fossils during expeditions in the Middle Awash region of Ethiopia in the 1990s that belong to a different species of hominid from Lucy. White named this hominid find from 2.5 million years ago *Australopithecus garhi.* "Garhi" means surprise in the Afar language. But to many scholars this discovery was no surprise.

They were expecting to find many different species of hominids living during this period. In fact, scholars will not be surprised to find more. What they weren't expecting to find were butchered antelope bones nearby. Here was the earliest evidence of toolmaking, meat-eating hominids. The bones of the antelope not only showed cut marks from tools, but had also been bashed with hammerstones to get at the **marrow** inside. White said, "All of a sudden this is a bipedal primate with a difference."

The discovery of *garhi* provided a piece to the puzzle from between 2 and 3 million years ago. White said, "You go into this period with, in essence, bipedal big-toothed chimps and come out with meat-eating large-brained hominids. That's a big change in a relatively short time. We'd really like to know more about what happened there." *Garhi* bridges the gap. How many other hominids do? With a lot of hard work, and perhaps a little luck, maybe we'll find more members of the family bush.

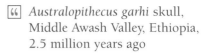

Australopithecus garhi skull, Middle Awash Valley, Ethiopia, 2.5 million years ago

Marrow is the soft, fatty material contained in the cavities of bones.

WHAT'S FOR LUNCH?

By studying Lucy's teeth and those of other hominids of her species, scientists have learned that they were primarily vegetarians. They ate seeds, nuts, berries, fruit, roots, tubers, and flowers. Their occasional protein snack probably came from bugs, lizards, and snakes.

CHAPTER 6

HOMO HABILIS
TOOLMAKING AND THE
HAMMERING HOMINID

The bus hummed along the highway. The scientists were worn out from the conference. Talk had wound down to murmurs here and there. Nick Toth sat in the back with his legs out straight, his arms folded across his chest, and his eyes closed. Sue Savage-Rumbaugh recalls in her book, *Kanzi*, that she thought he was asleep. So it startled her when he asked, "Do you think Kanzi could learn to make stone tools, the way early humans did?"

Kanzi, a bonobo chimpanzee, bashes rocks together to try to make a stone tool. It takes great concentration not to smash fingers.

Could he? Kanzi had amazed her time and again with his intelligence. And she knew that tool *use* was common in the wild. Chimps used stones as hammers to crack open nuts. They even made tools. They stripped leaves off branches to fish for termites. But pulling a few leaves off a branch wasn't even close to the skill it takes to make stone tools. Making stone tools was a human skill. Wasn't it?

Savage-Rumbaugh asked Toth, "Isn't stone tool-making a bit advanced for apes?" All the while Savage-Rumbaugh thought, what if? What if toolmaking turns out to be something Kanzi *can* do? When chimps were discovered making tools in the wild, scientists grumbled. They had to let go of the idea that toolmaking was uniquely human. It didn't take long for them to come up with a new definition that kept humans front and center. Using tools *to make* tools—now we're talking about a skill unique to humans. There's planning involved. You need big brains for that! But what would happen if Kanzi used tools to make tools? What made humans unique then?

Apparently Toth wasn't afraid of that question *or* the answer, because three weeks later he showed up at the research center with a truck full of rocks. Toth approached Kanzi's cage with an armload. Just outside the enclosure, he dropped the rocks, searching through the pile for the right two—two fist-sized rocks. Toth picked two rocks to knock together like our ancestors did at Olduvai Gorge in Africa. The rocks he chose would flake off into sharp slivers—sharp *knifelike* slivers. At Olduvai Gorge archaeologists found so many of these slivers, in so many different shapes, that they called it a tool kit and they named it after **Olduvai**. It is called the Oldowan tool kit. Toth wondered if Kanzi had the skill to make the Oldowan tools. Was this too much for an ape? Was this tool kit just for hammering hominids?

Inside his enclosure Kanzi wasn't concerned about the rocks. He knew what a rock was, but who was this man *with*

CANYON OF PREHISTORY

One of the most studied Stone Age archaeological sites is Olduvai Gorge. The gorge is a 30-mile-long, 300-foot-deep gash in the eastern Serengeti Plain in Tanzania. Ash from nearby volcanoes provided layers of protective coating. Today erosion is peeling away the layers. The layers of ash are easy to date, keeping a record of our earliest toolmaking ancestors and their tools.

" Flake tool, Hadar, Ethiopia, 2.3 million years ago

Olduvai, Olduway, Oldoway—all European stabs at what the Maasai herders call the Gorge. In their language it means, "The Place of Wild Sisal." Sisal is a plant whose fiber is often used to make rope.

the rocks? He bared his teeth. To Toth this may have looked like a happy grin, but Kanzi was anything but happy. Savage-Rumbaugh writes, "Kanzi considered Toth a stranger, and, as an adult male, felt it his duty to frighten away all 'outsiders.'" Kanzi made himself as large as possible. His hair stuck straight out. He screamed and charged the fence. He stamped his feet and charged the fence again, hooting, barking, and flailing his arms. Savage-Rumbaugh tried to convince Kanzi that Toth was a friend. But Kanzi would have none of it. He grabbed handfuls of cedar chips and threw them at Toth.

Toth picked up two rocks and began hitting them together.

Kanzi puffed up, hooted, and swayed from side to side.

Savage-Rumbaugh quietly spoke to Kanzi.

Toth noisily **knapped** rocks.

Flakes scattered. Rock chips flew. Cedar chips flew. Then suddenly everything was quiet. Toth put down what was left of his two rocks and searched for the sharpest flake in the debris around him. He picked a razor-sharp flake and used it to cut through the rope holding the lid in place on a clear plastic box. Inside the clear box was one of Kanzi's favorite treats—a juice box.

Kanzi watched. Hmmm, he liked what he saw inside those clear boxes—grapes, yum—watermelon, yum—juice boxes, YUM! Kanzi's hooting quieted to soft whimpers. Once things settled down and Savage-Rumbaugh convinced Kanzi that Toth was not a threat, she moved the tool-making materials inside the cage. Toth stayed outside, flaking stones. He passed sharp flakes to Savage-Rumbaugh inside the enclosure. She showed them to Kanzi. By the end of the day, Kanzi was using the flakes to cut ropes all by himself. This tool-using trick was great! The only time he forgot about his tool-using and juice-box drinking was when Toth got too close to the fence. Then Kanzi turned his attention to finding ways to grab Toth's shirt.

By the second day, Kanzi could tell the good flakes for cutting rope from the dull ones. Savage-Rumbaugh recalls in her book *Kanzi*, "several flakes flew off in different directions. Kanzi was watching closely and seemed to know

Stone knapping refers to the removal of flakes from a larger rock, called a core by archaeologists, by hitting it with another, smaller rock. You have to hit the core with just the right amount of force and at the correct angle to remove a flake.

which was the best flake, even before they hit the ground. He let out a **bonobo** squeal of delight, rushed to pick up the sharpest flake, and was off to the tool site with it, all in one fluid motion." He had even started bashing rocks together, trying to make his own tools. Savage-Rumbaugh writes, "Making flakes for himself, however, proved difficult...he seemed unable or unwilling to deliver a powerful blow. Bonobos are three times stronger than a human of the same size, so there was no doubt that Kanzi had the muscle power to do the job. We wondered whether he was nervous about hitting his fingers."

One afternoon a few months later, Savage-Rumbaugh was in her office when she heard BANG...BANG...BANG! She rushed to Kanzi's indoor room and, "there was Kanzi stone knapping with tremendous force. He had finally learned how to fracture rocks to make sharp flakes." Kanzi's tool-making abilities were extraordinary. He was bright, focused, and eager to get at the juice boxes. But how good were the tools he made? He wasn't even close to having the Oldowan hominid's skill. Kanzi's blows lacked the control that produced the flakes that Toth had examined at Olduvai Gorge.

Who *was* that hammering hominid at Olduvai? Just to make it crystal clear who that rock star was, scientists named him *Homo habilis,* which means "handy man." *Homo habilis* lived about a million years after Lucy's species, *Australopithecus afarensis.* How can archaeologists know for sure that *Homo habilis* was the hammering hominid? Well, he may not have been the only one. In fact, we're still not sure how many different hominids shared Africa 2 million years ago.

Another hominid often found at early tool sites is *Australopithecus boisei.* His cheekbones pushed so far forward they stuck out beyond his nose, giving his whole face a dish shape. On the top of his head, he had a ridge of bone called a **sagittal crest**. It looked like a bone mohawk. The crest wasn't a fashion statement; it was to hold muscles—muscles that powered his teeth. And this hominid had huge back teeth—really big—up to five times bigger than a human's. His jaws were so massive that he got the nickname

The bonobo is a pygmy chimpanzee.

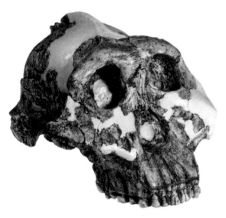

Australopithecus boisei skull, Olduvai, Tanzania, 1.8 million years ago

sagitta + *al* = "arrow" + "pertaining to"
A sagittal crest is a raised bony ridge that runs front to back on top of the skull.

Australopithecus boisei may have looked like this artist's reconstruction. If he lived today he'd be admired for those great cheekbones.

THE FIRST ROCK-BASHERS' CONVENTION

In Gona, Ethiopia, archaeologists have found some of the oldest tools and debris from their manufacture—nearly 3,000 pieces of worked stone. The tools are more than 2.5 million years old. Scientists believe the tools may have been used for digging up roots, butchering animals, and cracking shells and bones.

Nutcracker Man. You would think with such a big head that this was one tall hominid, but in fact, he only stood about four to four and a half feet tall. He spent his days chewing tough roots and bulbs. Could he have been a tool user, too? It's possible.

Even though stone tools look quite simple to make, don't let that fool you. They aren't. Savage-Rumbaugh wrote that Toth told her, "If a stone is merely slammed into another hard surface, with little regard for the angle of the blow, it may break, but it will have a battered appearance, looking precisely as though it had been battered. Well-flaked stone looks as though it had been sculpted or chiseled." Although Kanzi had come a long way from his timid taps, his tools still looked battered. He knew his tools weren't as good as a human's. Sometimes he would hold out two rocks for Savage-Rumbaugh to bash. Savage-Rumbaugh wouldn't do it for Kanzi. Kanzi thought about that. One day he just hauled off and threw a rock as hard as he could against the cement floor. It shattered. Flakes! Savage-Rumbaugh was excited about Kanzi's clever solution, but Toth wasn't. The Oldowan toolmakers did not make their tools by throwing. "If Kanzi throws the rocks, the . . . marks will be random, and we won't learn anything." They would never find out if Kanzi was capable of flaking stones with the same skill as *Homo habilis*.

How could they discourage Kanzi now that he was quite taken with this easy new flaking method? They covered the room with carpet. Kanzi thought about that. One day he pulled back the carpet. He hauled off and threw his rock against the exposed cement. It shattered. Flakes! Savage-Rumbaugh was tickled. Toth was not. Kanzi-2, Humans-0.

Many early tools look like something you would find in your own backyard. How does the scientist tell the difference between stones shaped by nature, called **geofacts**, and stones shaped by hominids, called **artifacts**? The earliest tools are often hard to tell from rocks that have been broken by natural forces such as glaciers and rivers. Scientists have to be aware of what the site was like long ago—was it the base of a waterfall? Often the motion of a glacier, river, or waterfall doesn't stop once the rock breaks; it keeps the rock tumbling—dulling and rounding the edge. Tools don't have this rounded edge. Still, it takes a trained eye to spot these early tools—and even the professional is not always sure.

If you know what to look for, there are clues. Suppose you find flakes, but there are no places nearby to get large enough rocks to flake. Someone had to bring in the big rock. Rocks don't walk. Or suppose the area where you find piles of flakes was once a quiet pond. What bashed the rocks? Or rather—*who* bashed the rocks? And then there are favorite rocks—rocks that make sharp flakes, such as quartz. Early hominids sometimes carried these rocks several miles. This just goes to show that—a good rock is hard to find. But ancient tools are not. Anthropologist Ian Tattersall tells us in Bill Bryson's book *A Short History of Nearly Everything* that hominids made tools "in the thousands. There are some places in Africa where you literally can't move without stepping on them. It was as if they made them for the sheer pleasure of it."

At the research center, spring had arrived, and it was warm enough to move Kanzi outside. The dirt would be too soft for him to use his rock-throwing technique. Kanzi practiced his hammering and got better at it. One afternoon Savage-Rumbaugh watched Kanzi sitting with his rock, thinking, when suddenly, he stood up and hauled off and threw his rock against a large boulder in the yard. It shattered. Flakes! It seemed that even though Kanzi might never be as skilled at knapping as the Oldowan toolmakers, outsmarting modern humans was no challenge at all.

geo + *facere* = "earth" + "to make"
A geofact is something created naturally by the earth.

arte + *facere* = "art" + "to make"
An artifact is something created by human workmanship.

CHAPTER 7

STONES AND BONES
THE OLD STONE AGE

Olduvai Gorge in Tanzania is only 300 feet deep, but it has been called the Grand Canyon of prehistory because of the depth of information provided by discoveries made there.

A savannah is an open plain where long grasses grow.

The truck bounced over ruts, rocking wildly. Kamoya Kimeu must have tried to steady himself as best he could in the bucking passenger seat. He and the others from his village were quiet. They were headed for Olduvai Gorge. They needed the money, but they weren't sure about this thing called a "dig." They did not want to touch dead people. Like many Africans, the Kamba believed it was bad luck. Thirty years after this bumpy ride in 1960 through the **savannah**, Kimeu told Virginia Morell when she interviewed him for her book *Ancestral Passions*, "We didn't know then about hominid bones, that there were such things. I thought we were coming to dig some graves of dead people. I didn't like that very much."

Kimeu trusted his uncle. If his uncle said that it was good work, it was good work. His uncle was traditional Kamba. His teeth were chipped and filed to sharp points in the ceremonial way of his ancestors, and if he said that this lady—this Mary Leakey—was to be trusted, then Kimeu believed him. His uncle might have yanked the wheel to avoid yet another water hole and sideswiped a sisal bush, its thorns scratching the side of the truck with a loud, scrreee.... Okay, maybe Kimeu shouldn't trust his uncle's driving so much. But everything else about his uncle? He trusted everything else.

At the camp Mary Leakey stood in front of the group of Kamba workmen, speaking to them in broken Swahili, part-English, and lots of sign language. She showed them how they would remove the rocks and dirt with picks and shovels. She showed them the little tools that they would use when they had taken away the top layer. Kimeu wondered how they would break through the rock-hard, baked clay with those tiny points.

Leakey took the workers to the area she wanted to excavate. They scrambled down the slope, the loose rock rolling under their feet. The dust rose up and made them cough. Leakey motioned to them to keep coming. When they were 10 feet from the bottom of the gorge, Leakey pulled out of her pack several wooden stakes. The Kamba stopped. Were they grave markers? Is this where they would have to dig up dead people? Some of the others must have inched back up the slope away from Leakey, who was pounding the stakes into the ground. Behind him, Kimeu would have heard the unsettled murmurs. As Leakey hammered, she explained that this was where they would dig the first trench.

Trench? Not grave?

Leakey probably reminded them of the food and the blankets that she would provide and the 10 dollars a month they would be making. The Kamba probably remembered that they were there because they needed the money for their families back home. So far they had not seen a dead person. Maybe it wouldn't hurt to dig rock and sand. It would be all right to touch the bones of an antelope. And so they dug.

NEW USE FOR OLD NAILS

The Kamba invented their own tool for breaking up the soil at early sites. They carved a wooden handle that fit nicely and felt comfortable in their grip. Then into the opposite end they hammered a six-inch nail, flattening it into a sharp chisel. The "Olduvai pick" is now in many East African archaeologists' tool kits.

At night the Kamba workmen sang songs and told stories around a campfire. Mary Leakey didn't join them. She sat alone at a worktable outside her tent, writing in her journal by the light of a lantern. She drew pictures of the fossils. She sketched the artifacts she found each day in the excavations. She wrote long letters to her husband, Louis Leakey, who was also an anthropologist. She planned the next day. She was there to work. Kamoya Kimeu watched her. She was so serious, this white lady. The days were long and hot. The Kamba crew removed tons of rock and soil. Kimeu told his interviewer, "We made a line with our shovels and picks and then we started digging. Then to make it go fast, we sang a Kamba song we always sing when we start to make a new *shamba* (garden). But Leakey said, 'What is this? This is not a potato *shamba!* Stop that singing!'"

Leakey wanted them to pay attention to what they were doing. She didn't want them singing. She didn't want them talking either. "*Yamaza!*" she would shout—"silence," in Swahili.

In the evenings the Kamba imitated Leakey and laughed. They strutted around the campfire, shouting orders in a

Mary Leakey instructs her workmen at Olduvai Gorge. The man on the far left is Kamoya Kimeu, who later was honored by the National Geographic Society for discovering more hominid fossils than any other person. The fourth man from the left is holding an Olduvai pick.

high-pitched voice. Kimeu glanced over now and again from the campfire where they spent their evenings to the worktable where Leakey spent hers. She was so serious, this white lady.

The Kamba women were not like Leakey. Leakey was *kali mzungu*—prickly white—and she was the boss in her household, not her husband. Not all the Kamba men thought that this was right. Many quit and went home. They did not want a woman to tell them what to do—especially this *kali mzungu* woman. But Kimeu did not quit. He stayed. He watched. He learned.

There were days when Leakey was in a good mood and explained to them why they were not to move the bits of bones and stones they found. She showed them how she pinpointed the location on a map of each fossil bone and tooth and each flake, core, and hammerstone. Kimeu said, "If Mary was not *kali* I'm sure we would not learn. So everybody was working hard, running hard, studying hard." No one worked harder than Kimeu and Leakey.

The crew dug. Leakey dug. They dug six-foot-wide steps, creating a staircase that went down four stories. The cut in the hillside revealed layers. The deeper they dug, the older the layers. In the middle, 20 feet down, they found the layer Leakey had been searching for, a layer nearly 2 million years old. Leakey called it the living floor. It was where the hominids had gathered.

The artifacts and fossils in the living floor were stuck under a thick layer of rock-hard volcanic ash. How could they get to them without destroying them? Leakey ordered the workers to pour water over the slab to loosen the ash. The workers poured gallon after gallon on the ash. But water is precious in the desert. The workers' angry murmurs grew into grumbles, then into loud complaints. Wasting water was bad luck. At night they stood in line for their water rations. A small cup was all that they were given to bathe. Meanwhile, Leakey ordered them to pour more water over the ash.

The volcanic ash began to loosen. The fossils and artifacts poked through unharmed. Leakey and the Kamba found

HOW DID THAT HAPPEN?

To reconstruct a picture of how ancient hominids lived, archaeologists must interpret a site by the position of the stone tools in relation to the animal bones, to the terrain, to the hominid. The archaeologist must piece together a picture of what was.

You've seen news reports on television in which people's homes are inches deep in muck after a flood. Stone Age areas have been covered in the same way. The problem with moving water is that it can disturb the evidence. Was this stone tool left next to this bone? Or has nature jumbled it all up?

As archaeologists strip the excavation layer by layer, they plot each find on a three-dimensional graph, then label and catalog it, keeping meticulous records. They are always paying attention to the relationship between objects and their environment, asking—is this how it was left a million years ago?

" Fossils and artifacts, Olduvai, Tanzania, 1.75 million years ago

Stone tools lie beside the bone of an extinct elephant in this block, which is just the same as it was when the Leakeys excavated it in 1960 at Olduvai Gorge.

3,150 large fossils, several thousand small bone fragments, 2,470 large stone tools, and 2,275 stone flakes. Leakey painstakingly labeled and mapped each find. This was the living floor. This was the place where hominids gathered nearly 2 million years ago. She hoped to understand what they did in this place by looking at what they left behind. Kimeu watched this serious, *kali mzungu* lady, day after day, for months. She scratched through the fawn-colored dirt, sketched in her notebook, and barked out her orders.

She seemed particularly interested in one area. It was an area where piles of smashed animal bones and many tools and flakes were scattered. Kimeu thought it looked like many animals had been butchered there. The sharp stones could have been used to cut through hides and carve animal meat. The more rounded stones could have been for smashing the bones to get at the marrow inside. Not far away was another area, oval-shaped, also thick with remains. Between the two areas was an empty narrow strip. Why was this strip empty? And why were there *two* groups of bones?

Had hominids gathered together to eat the meat of an animal they had hunted or scavenged? Leakey imagined them

EXTRA FAT WITH YOUR MEAT?

Wild game has very little fat, and yet, we need fat to digest protein. Hominids ate bone marrow because it is rich in fat. Carnivores gnaw and crunch bones to get the marrow, like a dog chewing a bone. Early Stone Age hominids struck thick bones with stone tools, breaking them open and scooping out the marrow inside.

making tools, butchering animals, and smashing the bones for marrow. Marrow! The bones in the oval area were bones that didn't contain much marrow—ribs, jawbones, and backbones. What if the strip had once been a line of bushes? The hominids could have tossed the bones without marrow over the bushes and kept the bones with marrow to smash when they had finished the butchering. From the bones left behind, Kimeu realized that hominids liked to eat antelope. The bones were not so different from the antelope he himself had hunted. But he also could see that they ate things that were easier to catch. They ate tortoises and chameleons and lizards and fish and snails. Kimeu didn't see any of the black rings that are left by a cooking fire. They must have eaten their food raw.

What *were* the hominids doing there? How were they using these places where they made tools and butchered animals? Were these home bases? When Mary Leakey excavated Olduvai Gorge in 1960, archaeologists thought areas containing bones and stones were 2-million-year-old campsites.

The hominids could have stayed at the campsite for a few days or several months. The group shared food and made tools. When the food became scarce they would pack up and move on to another site. Later, archaeologists worried that if they called these sites "home bases," then people would imagine a "home," when in fact there was no dwelling at all. They renamed them "central foraging places," hoping that name better described the way hominids lived.

Some scientists believed the sites were just places that hominids had found a dead animal and ate it. There was no food sharing. They just came across a carcass, smashed bones for the marrow, and then moved on.

Other scientists imagined the sites as tool storage areas spread around the hominids' territory. Hominids would carry a carcass to the nearest meat-processing place, where they kept a supply of stone tools. They would butcher the animal quickly, abandoning it before dangerous meat-eating animals, carnivores, were drawn to the area by the smells of the kill.

HOW TO SKIN AN ELEPHANT

Scientists experimented with stone tools to see what it was like to use them to butcher an elephant. (They experimented only on elephants that had died natural deaths.) Using a stone tool to cut through tough elephant hide is like slicing through a car tire with a razor blade. But once they get through the thick skin, the stones cut the meat easily. The scratch marks on the bones at Olduvai Gorge look like they were made with the knifelike edge of stone tools.

Louis and Mary Leakey and their son, Philip, excavate fossils and artifacts at Olduvai Gorge in 1960. Mary's dogs seem bored by the work.

Or maybe the hominids used the site because it was a good spot to butcher food, eat, socialize, and rest. They chose the site because it was shady, or safe from predators. There was no real plan to store tools—it just happened over time. One of the most difficult detective jobs that an archaeologist studying hominids has is to reconstruct how hominids lived. Was it picturing hominids so long ago that snagged Kimeu? Was it then that he caught the fossil fever? Or was it when he touched his first fossil? Perhaps it was that leg bone just outside the oval where hominids met so long ago—the hominid leg bone that was short and slender. When he touched it, he did not feel the dread of bad luck. He felt the thrill that he would find more.

CHAPTER 8

FINDING FABULOUS FOSSILS

TURKANA BOY

In his book *Origins Reconsidered*, Richard Leakey recalls anthropologist Alan Walker's explanation of what happened nearly 2 million years ago to Turkana Boy after he died. "The boy was lying face down in the shallows, head bobbing in the water. After a few days, or a week at the most, the flesh was putrefying, and the straight rooted teeth began to fall out." Walker speculates that "hippos and other animals wandered by, and the skeleton...got kicked about, the lighter bits going closer and closer to the shore. Something must have stood on the boy's right leg, because the fibula snapped in two, one of the pieces being pushed in to the sand."

For 1.6 million years, Turkana Boy's bones had lain buried on the west side of Lake Turkana in northern Kenya until a river called the Nariokotome began to wash away the dirt. A foot below the surface, the boy's sand-filled, upside-down skull held water and became the perfect pot to sprout a wait-a-bit thorn seed. Wait-a-bit thorns are hooked or barbed. When you brush past one of these thorn trees, they

Members of the hominid gang sieve sediment to look for small fragments of fossils.

Homo erectus skull, Turkana region, Kenya, 1.6 million years ago

snag your clothes, which means that you have to wait a bit because you have to carefully free yourself. For 20 years the tree grew. Its roots shot out, snaking between the plates of the braincase. The tree outgrew its pot and the skull burst apart. One small chunk of skull, the size of a matchbook, poked up to the surface. The bone was the same color as the lava pebbles scattered over the tawny dirt. For most of us, finding this bone would be exactly like trying to find a needle in a haystack. But the fossil hunter Kamoya Kimeu is not like most of us.

On August 22, 1984, Kamoya Kimeu felt restless. He sensed that hominid fossils should be on the banks of the sand river Nariokotome. The men Kimeu personally picked and trained had scoured the gullies for two weeks without finding a thing. They called themselves "the hominid gang" and they were not used to failure. If there were hominid bones to be found, these men would find them. They were the best. But the search so far had been a bust. Their backs ached. Their feet were sore. And their heads throbbed from concentrating for so long and so hard—from staring into the sand and squinting against the sun and heat that reflected back. The next day they would move camp. But Kimeu wasn't ready to give up. Not yet.

While the others wrote letters home, did their laundry, and boiled water for tea—comforting chores after weeks of little comfort—Kimeu began to walk. Walker tells us in his book *The Wisdom of Bones* what Kimeu remembered about those frustrating days. "You know, to walk continuously two weeks is too much. You go crazy, you can't think. So while they were resting, I just walked across to see how the country looked."

The second Kimeu spotted that tiny piece in the pebbles, he knew it was a scrap of skull—a hominid skull. And from the thickness, he knew it was a piece of *Homo erectus*—"upright man." Kimeu brought the fossil back to camp. The bad-luck streak had been broken.

When the anthropologists in charge of the expedition, Alan Walker and Richard Leakey, heard that the hominid gang had found only one tiny piece and nothing more, they assumed there would be no more bones. Alan Walker writes about how they felt, "Our hearts sank when we saw the small fossil, a rectangular piece about one inch by two inches, and the wretched little slope on the opposite bank of the river."

But archaeologists follow every lead, no matter how discouraging, so the hominid gang began clearing the site of all leaves, twigs, and pebbles and started the dusty, exhausting task of sifting the site. They broke up the top inch or so of packed earth with Olduvai picks. Once the layer was loosened, they shoveled it into wheelbarrows and moved it to the sieve. They tossed shovelful after shovelful of dirt onto the framed mesh and shook it back and forth and back and forth. After two hours of dust billowing and pebbles rattling and no discoveries, they were ready to give up. Just when everyone was convinced that that little piece of bone was all they would ever find, Turkana Boy surfaced.

For the next several weeks, the hominid gang dug up one extraordinary find after another. Walker wrote, "We made a detailed map of the excavation, recording the position of each bone to the nearest centimeter in three dimensions and drawing its orientation in the ground on the map."

While the hominid gang dug, Alan Walker worked with paleontologist Meave Leakey,

Anthropologist Alan Walker stands beside the skeleton of Turkana Boy. If this five-foot three-inch boy had lived to be an adult he would have been taller than Walker.

WHO'S WHO AMONG EARLY *HOMO*?

Scientists first found *Homo erectus* fossils in Asia, but the oldest specimens, including Turkana Boy, come from Africa. Some scientists think that these oldest African fossils belong to a different species, *Homo ergaster,* which means "workman." Turkana Boy is probably a descendant of *Homo habilis* or another species of early *Homo.*

A FAMILY AFFAIR

Three generations of Leakeys have caught a bug—the archaeology bug. Louis Leakey was born in 1903 in Africa, the son of missionaries. He and his second wife, Mary Leakey, led expeditions in East Africa, bringing their children along with them. Their son Richard found an important fossil when he was only six years old. Richard married a woman also passionate about fieldwork—Meave. Richard and Meave were the second generation of Leakeys to bring their children with them to the digs in Africa—Louise at only two weeks old. Louise must have caught that family bug, because she studied paleontology in college and then returned to dig in Africa on the west side of Lake Turkana, not far from where her mother put Turkana Boy's head back together again.

gluing the skull pieces back together. The two shared an unusual childhood habit. They both had loved jigsaw puzzles, but found them too easy. To make them more of a challenge, they used to turn the pieces upside down on the table and put the puzzle together without the picture. This turned out to be perfect training for recognizing shapes and a skill that helped them put Turkana Boy's skull back together even though it had been shattered by the roots of a wait-a-bit thorn tree.

Alan Walker writes in *The Wisdom of Bones*, that before long they knew that the find was an adolescent boy. "His browridges were fairly well developed for a youngster, meaning that, had he lived to grow up, he would have had the hulking browridges that decorate male *H. erectus* foreheads."

For the next four years, Alan Walker, Richard and Meave Leakey, Kamoya Kimeu, and his hominid gang spent each field season digging by the Nariokotome River. Turkana Boy's skeleton was so well preserved that they were able to learn more about *Homo erectus* than any scientists before them.

At eight years old, Turkana Boy was already five feet three inches tall. If he had lived to adulthood, he would have stood more than six feet tall. People who live in hot climates tend to be tall, like Turkana Boy. Over generations, tallness evolved in populations living in hot climates because a long body exposes a lot of skin to the air, making it easier to cool off. Height is not the only way Turkana Boy's body had evolved over generations to stay cool. Unlike other animals that pant to cool off, Turkana Boy could sweat. He had lost much of his body hair, and had developed a bit of a nose. Hominids before Turkana Boy had nostrils sunken into their faces. The nose cools and moistens hot air on the way to the lungs. If you can stay cool enough, you can be out and about in the middle of the day, hunting, scavenging, and foraging, when the only thing the other hunters are hunting for is shade. There is no competition for that delicious wildebeest carcass rotting in the sun!

Most animals' brains grow to almost full size before birth. Human brains, however, triple in size after birth. For this reason, human babies are dependent on their parents for a long time while the brain continues to grow and develop after birth. Turkana Boy's pelvis was small compared to his brain. Since the head must pass through the pelvis at birth and *erectus* had a small pelvis, it follows that there was a lot of brain growth going on after birth. This means that Turkana Boy's parents must have taken care of him and protected him while his brain continued to grow much like a human infant's parents would. And Turkana Boy's bigger brain—a brain half again as big as any hominid before him—gave him super powers compared to the other animals.

The spinal column is made up of a tower of **vertebrae** stacked one on top of the other like building blocks. Nerves run up through holes in the center of vertebrae. This collection of nerves, the spinal cord, controls the muscles in our arms, abdomen, and chest. The holes in Turkana Boy's vertebrae were narrow. He must have had fewer nerves in his spinal column than we do. The nerves that controlled his arms must have been there. The nerves that controlled walking must have been there. What's left? What nerves do we have that Turkana Boy didn't? Scientists think the nerves most likely to be missing were the ones that control breathing for speech. In other words, Turkana Boy could not talk. At least he couldn't talk in the traditional sense. But in his own way, he's told us a lot. Alan Walker writes in *The Wisdom of Bones*, "for the first time in history, we were able to look at an almost complete skeleton—not just a scrap of skull, a handful of teeth or a portion of an arm, but a bony record of one individual's life."

{ Vertebrae are the spool-shaped bones that make up the backbone.

66 *Homo erectus* vertebra, Turkana region, Kenya, 1.6 million years ago

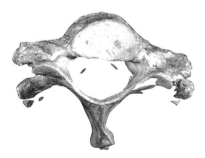

These vertebrae are from the Turkana boy (left) and a modern human (right). The space for the spinal cord to pass through the vertebra is twice as big in the modern human as it is in Turkana Boy.

CHAPTER 9

CONNECT THE DOTS
PEOPLING THE GLOBE

Homo + erectus = "man" +
"upright"
This is the oldest species to
be found outside Africa

If *Homo erectus* had learned to play a game, it would have been the one where everyone scatters the second the person who is "it" closes his eyes. Almost as soon as they appeared in Africa nearly 2 million years ago, *Homo erectus* spread out. They were hominids on the move.

Homo erectus looked a lot like us. Dolphins aren't as close to porpoises as we are to *erectus*. But don't let the similarities fool you: they were hulking hominids when it came to power. Anthropologist Alan Walker calls *Homo erectus* the "velociraptor of its day." And if you were to bump into one—run—because, Walker says, "you wouldn't connect. You'd be prey."

Just as we do, *erectus* walked with an upright, long-legged stride. It was a stride that carried these hominids over many generations across continents. Those legs took them up and

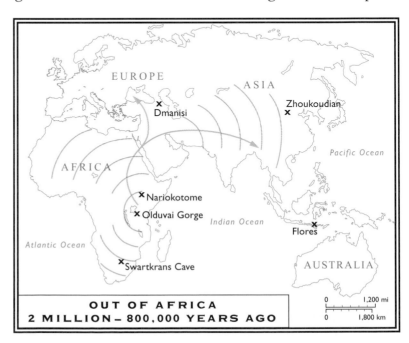

The arrows show the directions Homo erectus *migrated out of Africa. The arcs show how local populations spread outward over time as they grew.*

**OUT OF AFRICA
2 MILLION – 800,000 YEARS AGO**

down mountains, across deserts and rivers. That stride gave *erectus* hominids what anthropologist Ian Tattersall calls "a career as long-distance travelers." And, as Tattersall claims, *erectus* had the adventurous nature that is typically human. Their big brains helped them adjust to new climates, new foods, and new landscapes as they journeyed away from the familiar and into the unknown.

Anthropologist Alan Thorne explains how many other scholars see hominids moving out of Africa: "Humans came out of Africa in two waves—a first wave of *Homo erectus*, . . . and a later, more advanced wave of *Homo sapiens*, which displaced the first lot."

The problem in tracking the early hominids' exit is the lack of fossils. There are only scattered fragments from the scattering hominids. Alan Thorne points out how spotty the evidence is outside of Africa. "The whole of India has yielded just one ancient human fossil, from about 300,000 years ago. Between Iraq and Vietnam—that's a distance of some 3,000 miles—there have been just two. . . . It's not surprising that paleontologists have trouble connecting the dots."

Trying to figure out how hominids moved out of Africa and throughout the world is like playing a detective tailing a suspect. Scientists put together clues they uncover at digs and try to connect those dots. Most scientists agree that sometime between 2 and 1.5 million years ago, it was *Homo erectus* who got restless. *Erectus* started by spreading over most of Africa, then moved into southern Asia and finally the warmer parts of Europe. Here are a few of the scattered clues and the dots they may connect:

Clue #1 comes from Dmanisi in the Republic of Georgia, at the gates of Europe. Scientists found the skull of a trailblazing teenager who lived 1.75 million years ago. The skull and bones of at least five other individuals are the earliest evidence—so

> ## MOVING MOMENTS IN THE LIFE OF HOMO ERECTUS
>
> **1.75 million years ago**
> *Erectus* migrates out of Africa
>
> ---
>
> **1.25 million years ago**
> Fire used at Swartkrans Cave
>
> ---
>
> **800,000 years ago**
> Gran Dolina Boy migrates into western Europe; *Erectus* migrates over water

" *Homo erectus* skull, Dmanisi, Republic of Georgia, 1.75 million years ago

66 Tools, Dmanisi, Republic of Georgia, 1.75 million years ago

The tool on the left was excavated at Dmanisi. Hand axes such as the one on the right have been found with Homo erectus *fossils at other sites.*

far—of hominids outside Africa. The simple tools that they made from rocks gathered in nearby rivers were found with them.

The big brain that scientists expect to see in hominids, who needed it to figure out how to survive in new places, hadn't really developed for this primitive *Homo erectus*. But maybe they didn't need it yet. Scientists found African animal remains at Dmanisi, too. Ostriches and short-necked giraffes had taken the trip. When *erectus* made their way into Dmanisi it was a bit like East Africa, with its shrinking forests and expanding grasslands. The hominids and the animals were still in fairly familiar surroundings. Competition for food could have pushed these

Archaeologists hung strings from the roof of Swartkrans Cave in South Africa to form a grid. The lines help excavators map the locations of fossils in this limestone cave.

hominids farther and farther from home without forcing them to drastically change what food they ate or how they managed to get it. They could still get by without big brains. And now they had longer legs made for walking.

Clue #2 comes from Swartkrans Cave in South Africa. It was here that scientists found the bones to prove that we were not always the only hominid on the planet, as we are today. **Australopithecus robustus** lived alongside *Homo erectus* between 1 and 2 million years ago. That clue led scientists to understand that we didn't evolve in a straight line, one hominid evolving into another hominid into human beings, but that there were other branches of hominids. There were hominids not related to us—hominids who died out without a descendant.

As *erectus* spread into colder climates, they needed something for warmth. They needed **fire.** The first convincing evidence that a hominid actually used fire was in Swartkrans Cave between 1 and 1.5 million years ago. Someone—was it *erectus* or *robustus*?—grabbed a burning branch from a grass fire and brought it back to the cave. At some point they cooked part of an antelope—the world's first known barbecue. The hominid at Swartkrans didn't actually start the fire. Lightning probably did that. Total control of the flame was still a ways off.

Clue #3 comes from the underground tunnels and limestone caves of Gran Dolina in northern Spain. Some scholars call the hominids who reached western Europe 800,000 years ago *Homo* **antecessor**. Scientists named one hominid Gran Dolina Boy. He was around 11 when he died.

Australopithecus robustus skull, (part of the crest of bone along the top of this skull has broken off), Swartkrans, South Africa, 1.5 million years ago

Australis + pithekos + robustus = "southern" + "ape" + "robust"
Just to confuse you, this robust South (African) ape is a hominid, not an ape.

The earliest indisputable evidence of hominids fully controlling fire comes from hearths in Europe dating back 400,000 years. Scientists disagree about patches of baked earth on earlier sites. Were the fires started naturally by lightning? Or were they started by hominids?

Burned animal bones, Swartkrans, South Africa, 1.25 million years ago

antecessor = "one who goes before"
The anthropologists who named this species think it is the ancestor of later humans.

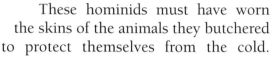

Homo antecessor skull, Gran Dolina, Spain, 800,000 years ago

Homo antecessor arm bone with butchering marks; Gran Dolina, Spain; 800,000 years ago

These hominids must have worn the skins of the animals they butchered to protect themselves from the cold. Thousands of butchered animal bones were found along with the simple flakes and chopping stones the hominids used. But these hominids were not only eating animals. Butchery cut marks were found on hominid bones. The marks show these hominids were eating each other. These are the first known cannibals.

Clue #4 comes from the Island of Flores in Indonesia. No one knows who lived there. Only tools remain. Scientists found the tools with the bones of an extinct pygmy elephant. Since that particular species of elephant was no longer around 750,000 years ago, the tools had to be at least that old. Scientists dated the layer of volcanic rock where the tools were found. The layer is 800,000 years old.

Up until then scholars had not found any evidence that hominids had crossed deep water before 50,000 years ago. So, finding 800,000-year-old tools—on an *island*—was a shock. Somehow hominids had crossed water to arrive on the

An artist drew this picture of Gran Dolina Boy from what his fossilized bones suggested he would look like. But we don't actually know what hairstyles hominids preferred.

Island of Flores. Did they lash bamboo together with reeds and raft across? Was the trip intentional? Or did they float over on a tree limb quite by accident? If it was an accident, we have one accident-prone *erectus*. The *closest* crossing, at the *lowest* of sea levels, requires *two* ten-mile-minimum crossings—from mainland to island—then from island to the Island of Flores.

Clue #5 comes from Zhoukoudian Cave in China. The cave is nestled in the mountains on the northern slope of Dragon Bone Hill. The *erectus* found there is called Peking Man. Peking Man lived about a half million years ago. Peking Man was named for the place this *erectus* was first found, which was near Beijing. This is not an evil plot to throw our detective off the trail of dots— at the time of the discovery, Beijing was called Peking.

66 *Homo erectus* skull, Beijing, China, 500,000 years ago

By half a million years ago, *erectus* hominids were showing off their big brains. China is a long way from where *erectus* started out in East Africa so many—about 125,000—generations ago. Along the way *erectus* must have met many challenges. New environments require new methods to survive. They couldn't have made the trip without the reasoning powers their growing brain provided. And with meat a major part of the hominids' diet, they no longer were tied to the plant life of a particular area. They were free to move, and move they did. *Homo erectus* ate whatever they could find—roots, berries, shellfish, eggs, nuts—and meat. We can tell from the wear on their teeth that these hominids ate more meat than their ancestors did. A big brain requires lots of energy, and meat is a high-energy food. It couldn't have been an easy life though. There must have

HOMINID HANGOUTS

Despite what popular images would have you believe, our ancestors were not cavemen. They lived outside caves more often than in them. Caves just happen to do a good job of preserving whatever is in them. The overhang protects whatever is inside from weather that might destroy it.

In the 1930s in Zhoukoudian, China, excavators carry a basket filled with rubble from the site to be sifted. The excavators mapped where they took each basketful according to the grid lines, similar to marking a box on a piece of graph paper.

been many hardships, many times of hunger, and lots of danger, because most *erectus* hominids never lived to be older than 14.

There is one mystery that our detective may never solve. During World War II, Chinese scientists packed up the bones of Peking Man and sent them off by train guarded by nine United States Marines. The bones were supposed to be loaded onto a steamer headed for the United States for safe-keeping. The train arrived at the port serving Peking the day the Japanese bombed Pearl Harbor. Amid the chaos of the war, the fossils were taken prisoner, and the bones disappeared. Years later, a mysterious American woman claimed she had possession of the kidnapped Peking Man. She demanded a ransom of half a million dollars. But when it came time to exchange the bones for the money at the designated location—on top of the Empire State Building—she ran. No one has found a trace of the mystery woman or Peking Man. Only the casts of the fossils remain to compare to all the other *erectus* fossils found since then—in China and along the many trails that connect the dots on the way out of Africa.

CHAPTER 10

ONCE UPON A RHINO TOOTH...
THE STORY OF HUNTING

O nce upon a rhino tooth? What happened to "time"? It turns out time *can* be told by rhino teeth. And our story begins with one.

If you imagine fog rolling in onto the beaches of Sussex, England, you probably wouldn't put a rhinoceros in the picture. But 500, 600, 700,000 years ago, they were there—along with a lot of other animals we think of as African. There were lions, bigger than any you'd find today, and elephants— twice the size of modern African elephants.

The hominids were big, too. The leg bone dug out of a chalky pit at an archaeological site called Boxgrove, in the hills of West Sussex, was massive. It belonged to our weak- chinned relative first found near Heidelberg, Germany, named *Homo heidelbergensis*. *Homo heidelbergensis* roamed Africa and Europe around half a million years ago. Their faces are the largest of all the hominids, their noses the widest. Their teeth were longer than ours and crowded

❝ *Homo heidelbergensis* leg bone, Boxgrove, England, 500,000 years ago

A group of Homo heidelbergensis *butcher a horse at Boxgrove in this artist's reconstruction. They probably wore skins for warmth and to protect themselves from sunburn.*

This rhino skull was found at Boxgrove. Without fire, the hominids ate the butchered rhinos raw.

their mouths. *Homo heidelbergensis* had no chins. But their brains were close in size to ours.

The leg bone found at Boxgrove must have come from a male. Hominid males are bigger than hominid females and the further back you go in our ancestry, the more the sexes differ in size. If this leg bone had been from a typical *Homo heidelbergensis* female, then she would have stood six feet tall and the male would have been much taller. He would have been a giant. Even though the animals at Boxgrove half a million years ago were big, they weren't *that* big. This isn't a fairy tale about giants. It begins, as we said, with a rhino tooth.

On a summer's day in 1986, the tooth was on its way to London by train. Simon Parfitt, Mark Robert's assistant director at the Boxgrove dig, was carrying it. Roberts writes in his book *Fairweather Eden,*

It lay inside his battered briefcase, wrapped in tissues in a plastic carrier bag. Of one thing, Simon was certain: it was a rhino tooth. And he knew enough about prehistoric rhinos to know that various species came and went during the long span of ice ages, which went from almost 2 million years ago to just down to 10,000 years ago. What he didn't know was how to tell them apart. Which was frustrating...

" Rhino tooth, Boxgrove, England, 500,000 years ago

It was frustrating because if he knew which species of rhino this tooth came from, it would give him a timeframe for the layer at Boxgrove where the tooth had been found.

Suppose you had a tooth belonging to King George. But you didn't know which King George—the First? Second? Third? Fourth? *Fifth?* If you knew the tooth belonged to King George I, you would know the tooth was from some time between 1660 and 1727, because that's when King George I was alive. Which is why Parfitt was on a train to London—to see a man about a tooth—a man who could tell Parfitt when *this* rhino ruled Sussex.

Scientists were in agreement that the species of rhino the tooth belonged to died out before the worst of the ice age known in Britain as the Anglian. Because the Anglian began around 480,000 years ago, this rhino tooth had to be older than 480,000 years. Scientists also agreed—at least they did in 1986—that there were no hominids in Britain until *after* the Anglian. The discovery of a single rhino tooth changed everything. The tooth was from the rhino that had died out before 480,000 years ago. And what else did they find in that layer at Boxgrove with the rhino tooth? They found hand axes. Hominids had made it as far north as Sussex half a million years ago—*before* the Anglian. They must have, because it sure wasn't rhinos whacking on rocks to make hand axes.

Archaeology is tough work in England. It's cold and wet and the finds aren't glamorous enough to make the cover of *Rolling Stone.* The winter after the archaeologists found the rhino tooth, the cold was so bitter that diggers lost feeling in their fingertips and their picks bounced off the frozen quarry floor. The workers had a bigger problem than cold—the rats! "They were everywhere," wrote co-author of *Fairweather Eden,* Michael Pitts, "in your sleeping bag, in your clothes, in the kitchen, perhaps, they joked, even in the stew—Mark shot anything that moved." But the scientists kept digging. They kept digging because

TIDES OF ICE

If we could speed up time and watch the expanding and contracting of glaciers from 1.8 million years ago to 10,000 years ago, it would look like tides coming in and going out. The Anglian would be one of many high tides.

Hand ax, Boxgrove, England, 500,000 years ago

Boxgrove is spectacular in the picture it draws of hominid behavior. We see how our ancestors lived off the land a half million years ago. But it wasn't glitzy and glamorous like some sites. In the limestone caves of Northern Spain at Atapuerca, something a whole lot flashier was getting attention. Even its name is more dramatic: The Pit of Bones.

The pit is at the bottom of a 15-foot shaft inside a hill. The series of chambers and tunnels was once home to cave bears. Among their bones, archaeologists found hominid remains— the remains of 32 *Homo heidelbergensis* individuals, mostly children, from 300,000 years ago. From the looks of things, the humans were thrown in on purpose. Did a disease wipe out so many? Was this a burial pit?

there were flints and animal bones by the thousands—by the hundreds of thousands.

They found so many hand axes they lost count. Hand axes are not like the primitive Oldowan tools found at Olduvai Gorge. A craftsman who worked with stone told Mark Roberts, "The ability to make a handaxe says everything you need to know about *Homo heidelbergensis*. People say it's just banging rocks together. But ask anyone who has to make a handaxe and you'll get a different story.... It's all planning.... It's like chess.... Sometimes you have to think five or six moves ahead. It takes months, if not years, to learn to do it well."

These were not dim-witted hominids at Boxgrove. These were chess masters. What were they thinking? How do you get inside the heads of the hominids who made these tools? What were they doing at Boxgrove? From the cut marks on the bones, it appeared as though they were butchers.

Scientists were amazed by how little the things they were finding had been disturbed. It had been half a million years, after all. Boxgrove wasn't like most sites, Roberts writes, "where rivers had jumbled everything together. Here the bones were perfectly preserved, so that the butchery marks could be seen even as you stood high above the trench floor. The flint axes were as sharp as the day they were made." In fact they were so sharp that the diggers had to be careful not to cut their hands when they removed them from the gravel pits. In one spot Roberts could see the outline of a hominid's legs where a knapper had sat making tools all day. The ground was littered with fragments except where the hominid's legs had touched the ground. Boxgrove looked as if it were under a spell, like Sleeping Beauty's castle—everything untouched until the prince came to

Skeletons of cave bears indicate that they weighed more than 1,000 pounds. Although the bears hibernated in caves, they spent most of their waking time outdoors munching on roots, berries, and other vegetarian foods.

wake her. Mark Roberts was the prince waking up Boxgrove. Boxgrove was coming alive again in the minds of the archaeologists who worked there.

66 Tool fragment, Boxgrove, England, 500,000 years ago

Roberts writes about how the bones revealed the ancient butchering process:

> Once the animal is down and dead, then the animal is skinned—there are certain characteristic cutmarks, especially around the head, that indicate skinning. ...After all the flesh had been cut and scraped away, the bones were smashed between a pebble and a flint anvil so the hominids could extract and eat the marrow. This, of course, would have been eaten warm and raw.

The meat would have been eaten raw, too. There was no evidence at Boxgrove that these hominids had controlled fire. But without fire, how did they keep the scavengers away? What kept the lions and wolves from robbing the hominids of their kill? These hominids didn't even appear to be in a hurry. Roberts estimates that at most 10 or 12 people worked together to butcher an animal. The same number of butchers today would take two or three hours to complete the work. Did the hominids chat while they worked? *Homo heidelbergensis* may have been the first hominid to talk. They wouldn't have sounded like we do because of the shape of their nose, but they were capable of talking. But did they? Mark Roberts thinks so. Something gave these hominids an advantage. It's clear they were not to be messed with—Roberts points out that even the hyenas that can heckle a lion away from its kill left the hominids alone.

Boxgrove shows a complete picture of butchery. Could it settle the argument scholars have debated for years? If Boxgrove could show how the hominids got the animals they butchered, scientists would be able to answer one of the key questions about hominid behavior. When did

THE OLD STONE AGE

Hand axes belong in a tool kit called "Acheulian," named after St. Acheul, a site in France where they were found. The period when Oldowan stone tools and Acheulian stone tools were being crafted is the earliest part of what archaeologists call the Paleolithic, which means "old stone." The Paleolithic lasted from the time of the first stone tools 2.5 million years ago to the end of the last ice age about 10,000 years ago.

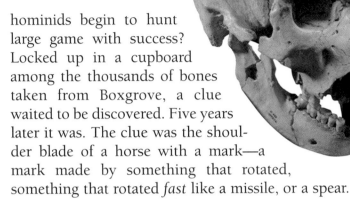

This skull from Kabwe, Zambia, comes from a species, Homo heidelbergensis, *that may have been an ancestor of the Neandertals and modern humans.*

❝ Horse bone, Boxgrove, England, 500,000 years ago

MEANWHILE IN GERMANY...

At the same time Boxgrove was being excavated in England, scientists were digging in Schöningen, Germany. The site wasn't as old as Boxgrove. It was from between 400,000 and 300,000 years ago. But a startling find linked the two sites. At Schöningen archaeologists found three wooden spears shaped like javelins. They may not have been the same style of weapon used to scar the horse at Boxgrove, but evidence for a hominid who hunted was piling up.

hominids begin to hunt large game with success? Locked up in a cupboard among the thousands of bones taken from Boxgrove, a clue waited to be discovered. Five years later it was. The clue was the shoulder blade of a horse with a mark—a mark made by something that rotated, something that rotated *fast* like a missile, or a spear.

The hominids hunted.

After a decade, the digging at Boxgrove was done. The work moved to cluttered tabletops in quiet labs. Cleaning and sorting and cataloging began. Years of study stretched ahead. Boxes of stones and bones are packed away in wooden drawers. There are hand axes made of flint. There's the long leg bone of *Homo heidelbergensis*. There are butchered remains of rhinos and horses and deer. Half a million years ago, these were not items stored in a narrow room in the natural history museum. That hand ax was someone's tool. That leg bone belonged to a man who looked out over the edge of the cliff watching the fog roll in. That shoulder bone with the circular scar was once part of a horse. They were all, as Roberts and Pitts wrote, "creatures that nuzzled and crawled and swam their lives in a landscape that we would recognize. Almost every animal we know today in Britain is there. The rabbits and robins and squirrels from our story books, the bears and wolves of fairy tales..." and the once-upon-a-rhino-tooth.

CHAPTER 11

WILL THE REAL NEANDERTAL PLEASE STAND UP?

NEANDERTAL—BEAUTY OR THE BEAST?

The rumble started from far away and grew—and grew. Like an ocean wave swelling with power, the rumble swelled with noise. The ground shook. Perhaps the scientists looked at one another wide-eyed, frozen for a split second before they broke loose from their shock, dropped their digging tools and scrambled for the walls of the cave. They would have pressed themselves against the rock, flattening into the wall, wishing they could sink into it, because in front of them it looked as if it were raining boulders. The ceiling of the cave broke up. Chunks of stone crashed down, cracked open, and bounced. The boulders rolled, slowing but not stopping, vibrating with the floor of the cave and the other fallen rocks. And then the rumble seemed to fade,

THAT'S TAL FOLKS...

You will on occasion see *Neandertal* spelled *Neanderthal*. The first bones of the Neandertal were found in Neander Valley, Germany. Back then, the German word for "valley" was *thal*. German has no "th" sound like in the word *thought*. In a language update around 1900, the Germans replaced all th's with t's. *Thal* is now *tal*. *Neanderthal* is now *Neandertal*. But no matter how you spell it, the last syllable is pronounced "tal."

This "model" Neandertal family lives in a cozy cave with a strategic view of the valley stretching out their front door. The lofty location gives them advance warning if uninvited guests try to approach.

Neandertal remains have been found only at sites in Europe and western Asia. The coastline is a little different from what you can see on a modern map because sea levels were lower during the ice ages, so more land was exposed during Neandertal times.

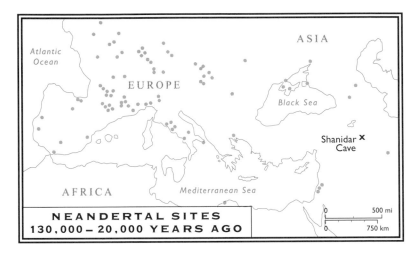

NEANDERTAL SITES
130,000 – 20,000 YEARS AGO

as if the wave had blown past them, moving farther down the valley. The scientists probably realized then that it wasn't the floor of the cave shaking now. It was their knees.

It was only then that they would have understood that it had been an earthquake. An earthquake! They were lucky. No one at the excavation was hurt. The ancients who lived here about 50,000 years ago had not been so lucky. Rockfalls killed at least four Neandertals in *this* cave, Shanidar Cave, in the mountains of northern Iraq. The scientist who led Shanidar's excavation, Ralph Solecki, wrote in his book *Shanidar* about one of the Neandertals he uncovered: "It was obvious to even the most casual of viewers that this was the head of a person who had suffered a sudden and violent end. The bashed-in head, the displaced lower jaw, and the unnatural twist of the neck were mute evidence of a horrible death." Solecki's own experience with the earthquake gave him a strong sense of how this Neandertal spent his last moments.

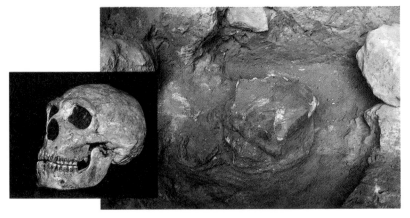

[66] Restored *Homo neanderthalensis* skull, Shanidar, Iraq, 50,000 years ago, and the site where it was found

But there were other Neandertals buried here. One in particular puzzled scientists. Soil samples taken from around his skeleton revealed an unexpected picture. This man, known as Shanidar IV, had been laid on a bed of horsetail branches in early summer more than 50,000 years ago. In his burial pit scientists found evidence of flowers— pollen from hyacinth, daisies, hollyhocks, St. Barnaby's thistle, bachelor's buttons, and yarrow. Here's where things start to get sketchy. How do we interpret this burial? Was the Neandertal a flower child? Or was he a beast?

❝ Flower burial, Shanidar, Iraq, 50,000 years ago

It's been said that if you gave a Neandertal a shave, stuck him in a suit and tie, and put him on the subway, no one would notice. The scientists who say that must be the kind of people who sleep on the subway or have their nose stuck in a newspaper, because you'd move to another seat if a Neandertal plunked down next to you. First there's his face. The Neandertal's face looked as if someone grabbed onto his nose and pulled the whole middle of his face out. The cheeks angled back to the ears. They weren't straight across like ours. Where we have a chin, the Neandertal's face sloped in. And those teeth were huge—much bigger than ours. The front teeth were worn down to stained stubs, probably from chewing on animal hides. Just above the eyes, shelflike bony browridges stuck out. He probably looked angry even when he wasn't. Then there's his body. Neandertals were sturdy—really sturdy. These stubby, barrel-chested, muscular hominids had thick bones built for abuse. If *that* sat next to you on the subway, you'd notice!

But as the saying goes, you can't judge a book by its cover. The Neandertal had a gentle side. In Shanidar Cave,

continues on page 78

WEIRD INTERPRETATIONS

In 1856 scientific thinking assumed humans came in one variety—us. So when a Neandertal skeleton was found in Germany, scientists came up with some peculiar explanations for this beetle-browed thug:

"It's a cave bear."

"It's the village idiot."

"It's a man suffering from rickets."

"It's a diseased cavalryman who suffered so much his frown bones grew large."

"It's a Mongolian soldier who deserted the Russian Army in 1814 while chasing Napoleon."

And the number one ridiculous explanation for the Neandertal's flat skull: "He clubbed himself over and over on the forehead."

ARCHAEOLOGIST AT WORK: AN INTERVIEW WITH OFER BAR-YOSEF

Ofer Bar-Yosef's love of archaeology began when he was a boy growing up in Jerusalem. He was only 11 years old when he rounded up a group of friends and excavated an area in the neighborhood. These days Bar-Yosef has no trouble rounding up friends and colleagues to dig wherever a puzzling problem— such as the demise of the Neandertals or the origins of agriculture in east and west Asia—sends him. When he's not digging, he's in his office at the Peabody Museum in Cambridge, Massachusetts, or in the classroom at Harvard University, where he is a professor of anthropology.

We understand you like to sample clam chowder wherever you go. Boston is known for its clam chowder; is that why you chose Harvard?
No, I came to Harvard because the university offered me some wonderful possibilities to do fieldwork in China, Republic of Georgia, Turkey, and other places. But I also like the food, and clam chowder is one of my most favorite soups.

You have worked many different kinds of sites. What can you tell us about the differences between excavating an open-air site and a cave site? And do you have a preference?
I have no preference because I choose the sites according to the problem which interests me. In both kinds of sites, you have to make decisions where to dig, how deep to go and so on, but especially with whom to work. It's nice to have colleagues who specialize in animal bones, geology, and other subjects to share the field experience.

Can you give us an example of a problem that interested you and the site you chose because of it?
After digging for 20 years in three caves in Israel and finding that Neandertals disappeared some 45,000 years ago from this region, I went to the Caucasus Mountains, where the rugged area would have been a good place for refugees, and got involved in two excavations. One is a rock shelter and the other one is a cave. Although we did not find the human fossils, I was able with my students and co-workers to demonstrate that Neandertals survived there until 35,000 years ago. This helps us to date the advance of modern humans, who came out of Africa, into Europe and western Asia.

One of your projects, Netiv Hagdud in the Jordan Valley, just north of Jericho, is called a pre-pottery village. What did they cook in if they didn't have pots?
They had milling stones and ground the seeds of wheat or barley and probably baked

them to make some pita bread. They also parched or toasted some other plants with small seeds. They roasted their meat from the hunted gazelle over fires, and used water bags to carry water and drink. But in similar bags they could have made some other drinks, such as a quasi-beer.

You worked on the Neandertal site Kebara in Israel. Some scholars think Neandertals were brutish and others think they were compassionate. From the evidence at Kebara, what are your thoughts?
I think they were probably both hard-living people but also compassionate. I cannot understand why they buried a dead man in the cave if they did not have some feelings about him. And we also know that hyenas visited the cave when the Neandertals went away for some time (perhaps two to three years). So they really dug a narrow pit and placed the corpse of this dead man and covered it well. When they left bodies of others such as young kids, the hyenas got them and we find only a few bones here and there.

Clues about our past come from many unusual sources. What did you discover from owl pellets at Kebara?
Owl pellets are common where barn owls live, and they refuse to share close neighborhood with humans; and this is why we call them barn owls and not house owls. Kebara was occupied most of the time by humans but when they were out for some years, owls found the small niches in the limestone walls a good place to nest. As they consume rodents, mostly during the night, we found lots of rodent bones in the pellets.

What information did the rodent bones give you?
The rodent bones tell you about the immediate environment of the cave, and the changes that took place during the many thousand years. Sometimes the area was a steppe with brushes and grass, and other times it was covered by oak forest.

If the car makers designed an ATV (all-time-vehicle) just for you, and you could travel back to any time and place in prehistory, when and where would you go?
I wish I could go to the time when a group of blond Neandertals in Europe met a small band of brown-skinned modern humans, who came originally from Africa. I would like to witness a real-time encounter, watch and listen if they knew how to talk to each other or simply spoke entirely different languages like Chinese and English. I am sure that they carried different hunting weapons and perhaps even used them to shoot each other.

What is the most exciting question about world prehistory to which we don't know the answer?
We have no idea how human mutations, and what kind, were responsible for the body we have now and in particular our brain size and construction. One of the great mysteries in human evolution is how we came to be what we are as human beings, and whether this is just an accident of the biological history of our planet.

GETTING STOMPED ON

Neandertal bones are evidence of a very tough life. They are riddled with injuries. Neandertals hurt their shoulders and arms, necks, and heads. Scientists observed the same injuries over and over in the skeletons that they were studying. The injuries followed a pattern—the same pattern of injuries seen in rodeo performers, who often get trampled when they fall off the animals they are riding. Scientists speculate that the Neandertal's hunting style caused the damage. Rushing in and jabbing a good-sized mammal with a thrusting spear doesn't really support the "smart" Neandertal model.

continued from page 75

one Neandertal in particular proved just how gentle. Ralph Solecki called him Nandy. He wrote, "the right arm, collar bone, and shoulder blade had never fully grown from birth." Nandy's right arm was withered and useless. Solecki continues, "Not only did he possess a disability from the day he was born, but he must have been blind in the left eye. He could barely forage and fend for himself." And yet, "he was accepted and supported by his people up to the day he died." Nandy died an old man—an old man for a Neandertal anyhow. From his bones and his teeth, we know he was about 40. It is not always easy to determine when an injury occurred. Some scholars believe that Nandy's arm was amputated later in life. Either way, he was cared for by other Neandertals.

Solecki's crew found Nandy the Neandertal under a pile of stones. A rockfall killed him.

A number of stones must have fallen on him within split seconds, throwing his body backwards... his body twisted to the right, pinning down his useless stump of a right arm. His left arm and hand, drawn protectively to his chest, were crushed into his ribs and spine. At the same time, a block of stone severed his head and neck from his trunk.

Some scientists argue that this reconstruction emphasizes the humanlike features of Neandertals too much—even without the suit and tie.

Solecki believes that the Neandertals who survived the rock-fall were grief-stricken when they found Nandy. Although not all scholars agree, Solecki believes they covered him with more stones and brought food as a tribute.

Were the Neandertals buried at Shanidar laid to rest with rituals? Were the mammal bones found with them part of a farewell feast? Did Shanidar IV's friends bring wild-flowers to his grave? Did they mourn his loss? Or, as some have suggested, did rodents scurry in with the debris? Did wind carry the flower pollen? Are we reading more into the burials than we should? Did Neandertals bury bodies just because they stank and would attract nasty bugs and beasts? Were the Neandertals noble? Or were they dim-witted brutes?

One thing scientists agree on is that the Neandertal was built for the cold. If you are cold at night, you curl up into a ball under the blankets. By compacting your body, you turn yourself into a little furnace pumping out heat and mini-mizing heat loss to the air. When you are hot at night, you stretch out on the sheets making yourself tall and exposing as much skin as you can to the air to cool off. Neandertals' short, barrel-shaped bodies did well in the cold.

The Neandertal's nose was a honker. Who would guess that a nose could be so important to survival? The Neandertals' giant schnoz did exactly the opposite of what you would expect. It dumped heat. Why would someone living during the Ice Age, in the coldest climate in which any hominid had ever lived, want to get *rid* of heat? Neandertals wanted to get rid of heat because the real danger in cold climates is overheating. If you overheat you sweat. And in extreme cold, sweat is a very dangerous thing, because it will freeze to your body and turn you into a Popsicle. Many scientists believe the Neandertal nose pro-tected them from sweating when they exerted themselves. Now that's a nose that knows.

If you love Neandertals, you might point to their big brains—bigger than our own in fact, and interpret the burials with tenderness. But not everyone looks so romantically on Neandertals. Archaeologist Lew Binford, who specializes in

NEANDERTALS AND THE ICE AGES

1.8 million–10,000 years ago
Geological epoch known as the Pleistocene—the period of the ice ages

About 130,000 years ago
Earliest Neandertals live in Europe

About 125,000–75,000 years ago
Warmer period during the ice ages; Neandertals also live in western Asia

About 75,000 years ago
Cold ice-age condi-tions return

About 50,000 years ago
Neandertals buried at Shanidar Cave, Iraq

29,000 years ago
What may be the last known Neandertal lived and died in Spain

"The first rule of anthropology is that if everybody believes what you've said, you've probably got it all wrong."

—Anthropologist Owen Lovejoy, in *Neandertal Enigma*, 1980

early hominid behavior, refuses even to call them human. Binford doesn't believe Neandertals lived in family units at all. He calls the ashy areas where they burned fires "nests." Because it was rare that the best cuts of meats were cooked at the nest, he sees the females and young getting by the best they could by foraging close to home while the males ran off to hunt.

Even Binford admits Neandertals used fire. In Shanidar Cave, stones that fell from the ceiling in the rockfall crashed into lit fires. Charcoal flecks are still stuck to the bottom of the stones. Solecki wrote, "Several fire hearths were contorted out of shape by the downthrust of the stones." Nandy was found buried beside two hearths, where Solecki believes Nandy made himself useful to his people. Maybe he prepared meals. Surely this separates Neandertals from beasts? Or does it? There is always the danger that we see only what we want to see, that we read into the evidence the conclusion we hope for. Was the Neandertal the gentle human that Solecki imagines? Or the animal Lew Binford pictures? Will the real Neandertal please stand up?

[66] *Homo neanderthalensis* burial, Shanidar, Iraq, 50,000 years ago

CHAPTER 12

BRAIN FOOD
THE MIDDLE STONE AGE

If the Neandertal wasn't "us," who was? Where can we find the first modern humans? A good place to begin looking is the southern tip of Africa in a place called Klasies River Mouth. This is not a place for the fainthearted, because one of the things Klasies people were eating 100,000 years ago was each other. Almost all the human bones found there were leftovers from cannibal dinners. They had been burned, torn open, and cut with stone tools.

Hilary Deacon, the archaeologist in charge at the Klasies site, describes what the marks on the bones tell us:

> Let's say that you want to heat up some brains. . . . You'd place the head on the fire. . . . When everything's nice and bubbly, you take it out. But you've still got to get the thing open, right? So you grab a hammerstone and give it a good bash. Naturally the bone is fresh and tears a bit as you pry open the skull. And that's where the tear marks come from.

“ *Homo sapiens sapiens* bone, Klasies River Mouth, South Africa, about 90,000 years ago

This bone is from the face of a modern human, Homo sapiens sapiens, *discovered at Klasies River Mouth. The cut marks at the top center of the bone are evidence of cannibalism.*

Cannibalism isn't uniquely human behavior. Many animals eat their own kind. The key question is why? If humans were eating humans because they were hungry, it's one thing, but if it was ritual, it's another. In some cultures, humans ritually eat parts of their dead loved ones, believing

DO YOU HEAR AN ECHO?

Our official name is *Homo sapiens sapiens.* "Wise" (*sapiens*) is not repeated to show off that we got a double dose of wisdom. It's to distinguish us from *Homo sapiens neanderthalensis* (Neandertals) and our earlier selves, which until recently were called "archaic" *Homo sapiens* (now known in Europe and Africa as *Homo heidelbergensis*).

WATCH CLOSELY NOW

Hilary Deacon was not the first person to excavate Klasies River Mouth when he began in 1984. Back in the 1960s, British and American archaeologists hot for hominids moved tons of dirt. Hilary Deacon's methods would have driven his predecessors crazy. His techniques are so exacting that they involve analyzing how individual grains of sand have weathered in order to estimate sea levels and climate.

that the best parts of their loved one's spirit—their courage, wisdom, strength—would be absorbed like a multivitamin. In other cultures, humans ritually eat parts of their enemies, believing it is an act of supreme dominance or revenge.

Anthropologist Tim White was quoted as saying in James Shreeve's book *The Neandertal Enigma,*

> If you are starving to death and you eat Uncle Harry, there is probably going to be some ritual involved. Even so, your motive for eating him was still starvation. On the other hand, there are societies where they eat Uncle Harry purely because they thought he was a neat guy and want to be a little more like him.

Why is it important to know if people were eating each other with or without ritual? Ritual cannibalism is proof of a complex belief system, which is modern behavior. Being a modern human isn't just about what we look like, it's about how we behave—how we think. Chimps and other animals may make tools, they may build shelters, but they don't perform rituals.

The Klasies people lived in these river-mouth caves in South Africa 100,000 years ago. The rocky coast-line of the Indian Ocean is just to the left, out of range of this photo.

So were the Klasies people starving or not? Is it likely? Klasies River Mouth looks out over open ocean. The gray-green cliffs rise up from the beach. The rocks tumbling out into the surf are speckled with shellfish. Birds nest in the ledges. Seals, penguins, and dolphins ride the waves. In the layers of debris left by modern humans, Deacon found shells and bones charred from being cooked. He said, "Klasies is the oldest seafood restaurant in the world."

In the ashes of the hearths, Deacon found that seafood wasn't the only thing on the menu. The people at Klasies ate plants and land animals as well. He found so many bones from a mild-mannered antelope, the eland, that Deacon thinks the herds may have been driven by the humans over cliffs or into traps.

Bashed-in bones alongside the hearths were marked by tools that were much more sophisticated than the tools used by *Homo erectus*. The blades were thinner and the way they had been crafted was more complicated. Some blades were made into points with blunted ends designed to attach to spears. Deacon believes that the evidence is mounting that the Klasies behaved like modern humans. Klasies people were advanced enough to control fire. They made fires for cooking, warmth, and protection. Deacon believes that they may also have burned the nearby vegetation. Were they advanced enough to plan for seasons ahead by recognizing that burning the old growth of the wild plants encouraged new growth? Were the Klasies people *that* modern?

What makes a modern human *modern* anyhow? Ritual cannibalism is an act requiring complex thought. It is symbolic. Crafting a varied tool kit is an act requiring complex thought. It is innovative. Altering your environment with fire is an act requiring complex thought. It takes planning. Whereas *Homo erectus* was controlled by his environment, modern humans took control of their environment.

Not all scientists agree with Deacon. Some say that the humans at Klasies were not modern. There is no evidence that they caught fish or flying birds. Herds of eland were so rare

CREATIVE THINKING

To some scientists, the people at Klasies are *near* modern. These scientists believe true moderns didn't emerge until 40,000–50,000 years ago when a burst of artistic behavior spread throughout the Old World. What caused this sudden burst of creativity? Some claim a change in the brain. Others say we just got better at talking.

Spear blade, South Africa, about 90,000 years ago

" Human bones, South Africa, about 90,000 years ago

These 90,000-year-old bones, including the jaw at top left, were excavated at Klasies River Mouth. They are among the oldest modern human bones in the world.

that they could not be counted on for a steady diet. But if the Klasies people were just living off what they could scavenge, you have to wonder how often dinner washed ashore.

If the evidence supporting modern human behavior isn't solid at Klasies, what about the anatomy of the humans living there? When it comes to classifying fossils, being modern *is* what you look like. Do the fossils at Klasies look like modern humans? If they do, at 90,000 years old, they would be the most ancient modern human remains found to date. Can we tell if the Klasies people were modern from a handful of teeth, chunks of jawbone, pieces of skull, and some shattered limb bones? The limb bones are delicate like our own. The jawbones for the most part show that the Klasies people had chins like we do. One skull fragment comes from the forehead—no browridge. All this put together convinces most scientists that this is indeed evidence of fully modern humans.

Scientists agree modern humans evolved from a human ancestor traditionally known as *Homo erectus*. It's the where, when, and how that start the disagreements. The clues are scattered all over the Old World, just waiting to be discovered.

EASY PICKINGS

Eland are by far the largest antelope. But some scientists argue that because the eland was the *only* large animal the Klasies people hunted, they were not truly modern. Remains of more dangerous animals—the Cape buffalo and bushpig—were from the vulnerable very young or very old, which were easy pickings. Fully modern humans with modern weapons hunt dangerous prey.

CHAPTER 13

I'VE GOT YOU UNDER MY SKIN
MODERN HUMAN ORIGINS

On Christmas Day 1998, in the Lapedo Valley, 90 miles north of Lisbon, Portugal, the steam shovel stood silent and still on the flat dirt terrace carved out of the cliff above the tree line. Its toothed bucket yawned at the base of the slope. The hillside was quiet now. Everyone had gone home to celebrate Christmas—everyone except the anthropology student, Cidália Duarte. She rolled onto her back, rubbing her elbow. Her left arm must have fallen asleep. She was trying to get the blood flowing again. Her arm tingled, and the smell of acetone, the chemical solvent she was using, made her dizzy. What was she doing here today? It was Christmas.

Duarte turned her head toward the four-year-old—the four-year-old who had been dead for 25,000 years. He lay on his back, too. She couldn't—*wouldn't*—leave the skeleton

❝ *Homo sapiens sapiens* skeleton, Lapedo Valley, Portugal, 25,000 years ago

Duarte's team had nicknamed "the Kid" out in the open. Anything could happen. Tonight the evening news would air the videotape that documented the excavation. Portuguese public television called the segment "A Child Is Born." Soon it wouldn't be enough to pull the old tractor hood over the Kid to hide him overnight. Soon they would need someone to protect him around the clock. The curious would come. They always do. She couldn't blame them. The Kid was *really* something.

The skeleton of the Kid as it was being excavated at Lagar Velho in the Lapedo Valley, Portugal.

He'd been buried turned toward the cliff with his right hand on his hip. His arms and legs were strong—built like

The Lagar Velho rock shelter in Portugal is where the Kid was discovered. Hominids and humans often camped in rock shelters because the overhanging cliff protected them from rain and wind.

a little boy's arms and legs. Duarte rolled back on her side and squirted acetone on the bone. It evaporated quickly, loosening the dirt but not damaging the bone. She picked up her paintbrush and swept the grit from his shoulder blade, and with a plastic spoon she gently scooped away the soil. It was a tedious process—a tedious task for Christmas Day.

Earlier she had found a pendant painted red, a tiny seashell someone 25,000 years ago had pierced a hole through to make a necklace for the Kid. She smiled, thinking of the human who made this necklace so long ago.

But something bothered Duarte. She knew it bothered the other scientists working here, too. There was something unusual about the Kid's combination of features. She thought of the Kid's snowplow-shaped Neandertal jaw and the pointed modern chin. Moderns found in Europe are called Cro-Magnons. They are named after the site where they were found in France. Cro-Magnon

66 Pendant, Lapedo Valley, Portugal, 25,000 years ago

people were the first *Homo sapiens sapiens,* arriving in Europe around 35,000 years ago. Could this be a child from both Cro-Magnon and Neandertal parents? The team took pictures and e-mailed them to an authority on early modern anatomy whose specialty was Neandertals.

Like almost anything archaeologists dig up, the Kid caused a stir in the scientific community. Scientists who supported a theory that modern humans—humans like us—had come out of Africa and *replaced* populations along the way did not want to hear about a hybrid child. Their story—known as Out of Africa—had fully modern humans leaving Africa and spreading across Europe and Asia. The new arrivals drove existing populations to extinction. There was no mixing of populations in their theory. It was out with the old, in with the new.

There have been many theories as to how the Neandertals ended their time on Earth. Some suggested that Cro-Magnons massacred the Neandertals, or pushed them out of their hunting grounds and into nooks where they could do little more than scratch out a pitiful existence. Others said that the Cro-Magnons were carriers of deadly viruses to which the Neandertals had no immunity. But the Cro-Magnon takeover didn't have to be so dramatic. As the science writer James Shreeve explains in *The Neandertal Enigma* about the Cro-Magnons, "They had only to produce a few more babies every year than the beetle-browed others they occasionally met and after a couple of thousand years, the job was done." Many anthropologists agree, suggesting that instead of a climactic last scene, Neandertals simply faded out.

And then there were those who don't buy into this Out of Africa business. These scientists believed that populations all over the Old World evolved into modern humans gradually about the same time. To these scientists, Neandertals are not just some dead-end population replaced by a new and improved version. For them the Kid represents a step along the path from old to new.

There was no question that by 35,000 years ago, moderns were springing up all over the Old World. The question was— *how?* Did the moderns evolve from existing populations?

NEW MEANING TO THE TERM "GYM RAT"

Some scientists go to extremes in the name of science. One extreme scientist wanted to prove that Neandertals' bones were thicker than those of modern humans not because of their genes, but because their lifestyle was so much more active. For hours every day he made armadillos jog on treadmills to prove his point. He chose armadillos because they have litters of four genetically identical young. Two he would let go about their normal digging ways, and two would hit the gym. The running armadillos always had thicker bones— the more exercise, the thicker the bones.

Or were moderns moving in? One winter in 1970 a young man named Chris Stringer decided to find out. He had no money and no reputation (yet), but he had a passion. The passion began when he was nine years old and he heard a BBC radio show about Neandertals called "How Things Began." At 10 he was sketching skulls. At 11 he was following a teacher to digs. His parents thought that this was a bit odd, but they figured that he'd grow out of it and come to his senses.

"By sixteen, I was on track for medical school," Stringer told author James Shreeve, who interviewed him for the book *The Neandertal Enigma.* "And then somebody handed me a college catalog, and I saw a course listed under 'Anthropology.' Until that moment, I had no idea that you could actually do this for a living."

In graduate school he began his quest for the answer to modern human origins. He thought that if he could just measure enough skulls, he would find out if Neandertals evolved into modern humans or if they were two separate twigs on the evolutionary bush. Chris Stringer writes in his book *African Exodus,*

I would use precise instruments such as calipers and protractors to determine skull height, breadth, and width; angle of forehead; projection of browridge;

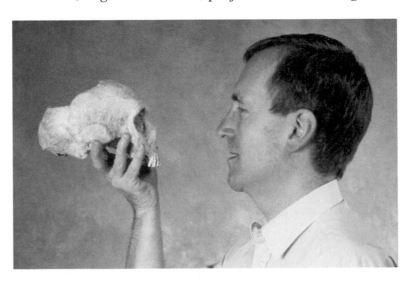

Nose to nose: paleoanthropologist Chris Stringer examines a hominid skull (or is it the other way around?).

and dozens of other features to place Neanderthals and Cro-Magnons in their evolutionary context.... All that concerned me...was getting my hands on fossil skulls—many of which could be found in European museums where they had been gathering dust since the turn of the century.

Chris Stringer traveled across Europe sleeping in his car, camping, or staying in youth hostels. He measured Neandertal skulls wherever museums and universities would let him. In Rome thieves broke into his car. They took his clothes and a fresh human skull he'd brought along to compare to the Neandertal skulls he was measuring. He writes, "My precious measuring instruments and hard won data were not stolen. If I had lost these, I would—as I recorded in my diary—have simply thrown myself in the [River] Tiber. From then on, I always slept with my data sheets under my pillow."

At the end of his journey, he had run out of money and clean clothes. He'd lost 14 pounds and his car was held together with coat hangers. But he had measured his way to an answer that satisfied him, if not other scientists. He writes, "I became convinced the Neanderthals were not our ancestors,...and that there was little sign of intermixture between Neanderthals and early modern people."

Chris Stringer has come a long way from the days of sleeping in his car. Students approach him now and ask his permission to examine hominids at the Natural History Museum in London. So what does Chris Stringer make of the Kid—the intermixture of which he claimed there was little sign? He doesn't want to jump to conclusions. He entertains all explanations, including climate, for the Kid's sturdy bones. It is entirely possible that the Kid is completely modern, with no Neandertal in him at all. After all, look at *us*. We look very different from one another. Stringer writes, "Human differences are mostly superficial. What unites us is far more significant than what divides us. Our variable forms mask an essential truth—that under our skins, we are all Africans."

RACE?

Race is a scientific term that came about when scientists observed that a plant growing in the north may express itself differently from the same plant growing in the hot, humid south. Race is an attempt to group these differences. There are problems with racial groupings, particularly when it comes to humans. One obvious feature that varies from human to human depending on geography is skin color.

Near the equator, where the sun is strong, humans have dark skin. Dark skin protects the body from too much ultraviolet light. Skin color changes very gradually as you travel away from the equator and the sun's rays lose their intensity. People in places like North Africa and southern Europe have brownish skin; they are neither black nor white. Many scientists believe race is meaningless when applied to humans.

CHAPTER 14

DUCK HUNTING—RUN!
THE PEOPLING OF AUSTRALIA

WHALE'S NOT SAYING WHEN

No one knows exactly when Australia was settled. Growing archaeological evidence indicates that the first people arrived more than 40,000 years ago, but how much earlier is a matter of debate.

The true natives of Australia, the Australian Aborigines, hand their ancestors' stories down from one generation to the next. The stories reach all the way back to the Aborigines' origins, a time they call the Dreamtime. One Dreamtime story tells about how the first people came to Australia. It begins as many stories do—long, long ago.

And it *was* long ago. The first people must have come more than 30,000 years ago, because by then Australia had been settled. Pinpointing exactly when the first people stepped onto Australian soil is not easy. It's not as if archaeologists discovered a headstone marked "I was here first!" The archaeologists aren't sure if the bones that they are finding are bones from the first people to come to Australia or bones from people whose ancestors had come to Australia thousands of years before.

One thing that muddies the picture is that sea levels back then were very low. The water levels had dropped so low that New Guinea and Tasmania, which are now islands off the coast of Australia, were joined to the Australian mainland. What was coastline then is underwater now. And since it is likely that the first people to come to Australia settled along the coast, evidence of them is going to be hard to find.

One Dreamtime story tells how the first people came to Australia from a land beyond the sea. Forty thousand years ago, humans couldn't

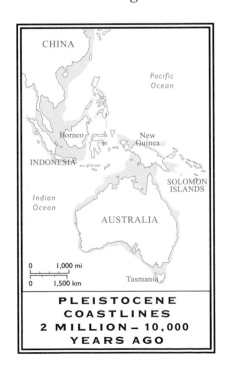

CHINA

Pacific
Ocean

Borneo

New
Guinea

INDONESIA

SOLOMON
ISLANDS

Indian
Ocean

AUSTRALIA

0   1,000 mi
0   1,500 km

Tasmania

**PLEISTOCENE
COASTLINES
2 MILLION–10,000
YEARS AGO**

During the ice ages, sea levels were lower than they are now, so Australia was joined to New Guinea and Indonesia to the Asian mainland. However, humans must still have ventured across the seas to reach Australia for the first time.

have survived a sea voyage from India, China, or Africa. But they could have island-hopped from Southeast Asia. The earliest people to come to Australia probably used the island pathway like stepping stones, sailing or paddling from one island to the next. According to the Dreamtime story, the first people came looking for better hunting grounds:

> They knew the voyage would be a long and danger-ous one; storms would sweep across the sea and lash the waves into a white fury; the wind would howl like the evil spirits of the forest, the lightning flash across the sky like writhing golden snakes, and death would hide in waiting for them beneath the brown sea kelp. It was therefore necessary for them to have a very strong canoe for the journey.

The largest and sturdiest canoe belonged to Whale. But Whale was not very generous. He would not let anyone use his giant canoe. No one else had a canoe big enough to make the trip to Australia. They needed Whale's canoe. Koala and Bird began to watch Whale's canoe in the hope that he would leave it long enough for them to steal. But Whale guarded his canoe closely.

As with most legends, truths are buried in the tale. The first Australians would have needed a sturdy boat to survive the 50 or more miles between islands to get to Australia. Flimsy rafts or unstable small canoes would have most likely sunk.

Eventually, thanks to Starfish's devious plan to distract Whale by picking lice from his head, the others were able to snatch the canoe and make for Australia. When Whale found out that Koala and Bird had stolen his canoe he was so mad that he and Starfish had a fight. That's how Starfish got tattered. But Whale didn't get away unhurt. Starfish punched a hole in his head. That's why today you see whales spout through their blowhole—all right, so not everything buried in legends is true.

The Dreamtime stories that come from ancient memories tell tales of rising seas, of climate change that turned lush land to desert, and of a time when giant beasts roamed Australia. You might hear an Australian say he is Kangaroo

TRACKING TRADE

Early people exchanged toolmaking materials. One valued stone—obsidian—has been found on many islands in the Pacific. Because obsidian can only be gathered from a very few locations, it is clear that it was traded through-out the Solomon Islands.

" Aboriginal Dreamtime story, Australia, date unknown

"Demon ducks of doom," the giant flightless birds Genyornis newtoni lived in Australia when humans arrived. They stood more than six feet tall. Look at that huge, powerful beak in this artist's reconstruction; Genyornis means "jaw bird."

This skeleton belongs to an extinct giant wallaby, a close relative of the kangaroo. It was a marsupial, an animal whose young is nursed in a pouch.

Dreaming or Wombat Dreaming...or *Giant Duck Dreaming?* This is a case where we know the Dreamtime story *is* true. When the first people paddled ashore, they were met by strange animals—animals that had evolved in isolation for millions of years.

Australia had once been home to giant beasts—GIANT beasts. There were kangaroos as big as houses, tortoises the size of cars, snakes twenty-five feet long and three feet around, and lizards that would barely fit in your classroom. But without a doubt, the scariest, most ferocious of all was the giant man-eating duck (well, it could have hunted humans, it ate meat and hunted large mammals). The scientists at the Australian museum studying a duck skull that was found in the Northern Territory at Bullock Creek have nicknamed the giant bird "the demon duck of doom." With a beak the size and shape of an ax, you can understand how it got that name.

By the time the first Australians arrived on the scene, the animals may have downsized a bit, but they were still freakishly gigantic. So what happened to these giant beasts? That's a good question. Scientists don't know if they disappeared because humans arrived or because the climate changed. It would help if scientists knew how long ago humans came to Australia and when the **megafauna** left. Until they know for sure, scientists will argue: Did the early settlers hunt the giant beasts into extinction? Did they set fires to promote plant growth for their own food only to burn off everyone else's dinner? Or when the climate changed and Australia dried up, did the land stop supporting dino-sized ducks? Maybe it was a bit of all three?

As for the ending of the Dreamtime story about the first people to arrive in Australia, it goes like this: when Whale's canoe got to Australia, Bird was so excited that he jumped up and down punching two holes in the bottom of the bark canoe. It sank. Whale was furious. He can still be seen swimming back and forth offshore, spouting through his blowhole. Maybe he's not angry. Maybe he's afraid of the duck.

mega + *fauna* = "large" + "all the animals in one region or period of time"
The megafauna are all the large animals in one area, in this case Australia.

ISLAND HOPPING

The Solomon Islands were settled by people who went on a long sea voyage 30,000 years ago. The only way people could have arrived on these islands was by some sort of watercraft.

CHAPTER 15

ON THE WAY TO THE MALL
COMPLEX PALEOLITHIC TECHNOLOGY

Stand in the middle of any mall in the United States or any main street in any city in the world and look around—so much *stuff!* For thousands and thousands of years, the only thing we can prove that humans possessed were chunks of stone they whacked into a crude shape roughly resembling what we'd call tools. Now look. When on earth did everything change?

From the time *Homo habilis* first smacked two stones together until nearly 45,000 years ago, the list of artifacts is pretty monotonous—stone tools and more stone tools. Only an archaeologist could get excited about the "new developments" in tool technology happening back then—oh, look, they're chipping off both sides of the rock now—*wow!* But then sometime around 45,000 years ago, *something* did change. Artifact lists begin to rival hardware store inventories—from fishhooks to sewing needles. Even the materials changed. Tools made from stone for thousands of generations were now being carved out of antler, bone, and ivory. Improvements on old tools were happening quicker than you can say "holy hunting hominids!" Blade edges were sharper. Toolmakers were getting more flakes from a single stone with new techniques. Handles were attached to tools. Handles may seem like a simple addition, but that single change had an enormous impact on lifestyle. Imagine an ax without its handle. Now imagine cutting down a tree. Easier with the handle, don't you agree?

Sometimes simple changes can make all the difference. Take spears, for example. Most spears had been designed for thrusting. The hunter ran up to the nearest nasty-tempered beast and jabbed him with his spear. Undoubtedly, the beast

REGIONAL DIFFERENCES

At one time "stuff" looked pretty much the same all over the Old World. A hide scraper from South Africa looked much the same as a hide scraper from East Asia. A creative explosion marked the beginning of regional differences. Today we have chopsticks and silverware, saris and blue jeans, rickshaws and taxicabs. Travel to anywhere in the world, and chances are you will find clues to your location by the "stuff." Where might you be if you are wearing a beret? A ten-gallon hat? A sombrero? A turban?

TRAIL OF TURDS

Prehistoric artists carved images into practical objects. One artist carved an image of a wild goat into the end of a spear-thrower. The wild goat's rump was lifted in the air eliminating a giant turd. Was the artist trying to be funny? Or is the turd coming out of the goat's rump a message to hunters? "Follow the trail of turds that look like this and eventually you will find the goat."

66 Harpoon, Anège, France, 20,000–10,000 years ago

would be unhappy about this. Getting close enough to jab a grumpy woolly rhino with a horn as long as your spear clearly had its drawbacks. The new spears, from sometime around 30,000 years ago, were lighter, designed to be thrown from a safe distance. Simple change, enormous consequence—hunting instantly became much safer.

Not all changes were quite so simple. Take the spear-thrower, for example. The spear-thrower, which looks like a giant crochet hook, acted like an extension of the hunter's arm, increasing the force of the throw. With it the spear could be hurled longer distances at fast-moving, skittish prey that had previously been difficult to hunt. The greater force of impact made the spear all the more deadly. Even the spear points began showing advancements. Hunters discovered that if they barbed the point, the spear would stay lodged in the beast. And if they cut a groove in the point, it increased the blood flow out of the wound, which weakened the animal faster.

Weapons weren't the only things that were new and improved. Hunting methods were changing as well. Impressions of woven and knotted cords found in clay at Dolní Věstonice, an Ice Age hunters' site in the Czech Republic, led scientists to believe the women and men had begun hunting with nets. In France there is a kill site where prehistoric hunters drove hundreds of horses over a cliff. In coastal communities, hunters hurled harpoons at whales, exploiting sea life in new ways—humans were fishing. The very first stories about "the one that got away" must have begun in those evenings by the fire.

Initially archaeologists thought the 100 or so Cro-Magnon people who settled 27,000 years ago on the edge of a swamp at the site now known as Dolní Věstonice had come to hunt **mammoth**. But many archaeologists now think it was not the mammoth that drew the hunters, but the mammoth bones. At a nearby watering hole, as the beasts died, over time the bones accumulated. The Cro-Magnon people used the mammoth bones for many things. They splintered the bones for sewing needles, carved the bones into a variety of tools, built shelters using the bones as a framework, and when wood was scarce, they burned the bones for warmth.

On the grassy hillside near Dolní Věstonice, the Cro-Magnons built five huts and surrounded them with a fence made of mammoth bones and tusks stuck into the ground. In the fence's crevices, they stuffed brush and turf, creating a windbreak and a barrier against predators. To further discourage dangerous animals, the Cro-Magnons kept a fire

{ The mammoth was a very large elephantlike mammal, typically hairy with a sloping back and long curved tusks, which became extinct during the last Ice Age but are known from fossil remains, frozen carcasses, and Paleolithic drawings.

Mammoth bones form the framework of a hut in this reconstruction. Skins probably covered the bones to block out wind and snow. Five similar huts dating to 15,000 years ago were found at Mezhirich, in the Ukraine.

burning. Its warmth was probably welcome in the freezing Ice Age temperatures. The huts were constructed like giant tents, with wooden posts leaning toward the center and animal skins draped over the frames and anchored to the ground with stones and bones. The largest of the huts had five shallow hearths for cooking, one equipped with a rotisserie made from mammoth bones.

One hut stood far from the others. Its hearth was not for cooking. The dome-shaped hearth was used as a kiln for baking clay. The Cro-Magnon artist mixed clay from earth and powdered bone and then shaped it. The floor of the sculptor's hut was covered with bits and pieces of ceramic animal heads—wolves, bears, and foxes. In some of the lumps of clay, you can still see the fingerprints of the artist.

66 Clay animals, Dolní Věstonice, Czech Republic, 27,000 years ago

But it is a second kiln that has archaeologists scratching their heads. They found thousands of bits and pieces that had been broken not by accident, or over time, but deliberately. It seems the Cro-Magnons were placing statues of women in the hottest part of the fire and watching them explode. Archaeologist Olga Softer tells *Discover* magazine, "Either we're dealing with the most inept potters, people with two left hands, or they are doing it on purpose." She suggests perhaps they blew up the figures in a ceremony to predict the future. "Some stuff is going to explode. Some stuff is not going to explode. It's . . . like picking petals off a daisy. She loves me, she loves me not."

Up until this time in prehistory, the majority of items on site lists had been directly related to survival, such as butchering tools and hunting weapons. But now, items such as the exploding figurines were beginning to show up. The catalog of items at Sunghir, a burial site near Moscow, Russia, the same age as Dolní Věstonice, is pages long. In one grave archaeologists found jewelry—bracelets, necklaces,

PART OF THE OLD STONE AGE

The last part of the Paleolithic in Europe is the Upper Paleolithic, which lasted from about 40,000 years ago down to the end of the last Ice Age, about 10,000 years ago.

pendants, and *10,000* beads carved from ivory. The pattern of beads across the forehead and chest and down each leg makes archaeologists think the beads were sewn into what was once clothing before it disintegrated, perhaps a hooded tunic and pants. Each of the beads must have taken at least one hour to make, that's *10,000 hours* making beads. Humans were on their way to the mall.

Homo sapiens sapiens skeleton, Sunghir, Russia, 28,000 years ago

Why this change? What was so different about humans after 45,000 years ago? Why do we find only clunky stone tools for thousands and thousands of years and then all this stuff? Some scientists argue that the brain changed; others say it's all about language. If the brain changed, there is no evidence of it. There are no marks on the inside of skulls that show a brain change occurring at the same time as this astounding variety of possessions. And if there had been a biological event such as a new and improved brain, you would expect to see creativity blossom outward from the one location where this brainy bunch lived. Instead, creativity seemed to be sparking all over the Old World like bursts of fireworks in the sky.

What about language? Could words have warped the world? Many scientists believe that Neandertals were capable of language and yet their creative endeavors were limited. If language was the root of this flurry of new inventions and artistic expressions, why weren't the Neandertals in on it?

Is the answer at Dolní Věstonice? Maybe we should put a Venus figurine in the fire and see if it explodes. If it does, it's a brain change. If it doesn't, it's language.

MESSAGES FROM THE GRAVE

In 1986 the bodies of three teens were found buried together at Dolní Věstonice. There were two boys and one girl—at least that's what some think; others think three boys. The young girl's spine was badly deformed, and one of the boys had a wooden pole thrust through his hip. The girl rested between the two boys, one reaching out to her, and the other linking arms with her. All three had been dusted with red pigment. Had someone carefully arranged these bodies 28,000 years ago? Or were they tossed in the common grave, and archaeologists are trying to read messages that aren't there?

CHAPTER 16

CRAWLING THROUGH CAVES

ROCK ART

December 18, 1994, three o'clock Sunday afternoon on a cliff-side in France: He wasn't sure which he felt first, the puff of air against his cheek or the hair standing up on the back of his neck. Jean-Marie Chauvet stopped so suddenly that Christian Hillaire and Eliette Brunel Deschamps bumped into him. Chauvet looked at his friends. Had they felt something, too? The three studied the limestone rock face that rose up on their right. There—up there, just above their heads—an opening. Deschamps closed her eyes and lifted her face to the black hole. Yes, she felt it, too—faintly, but it was there: cool humid air blowing from between the boulders. Air flowing from animal burrows—from any crack or crevice—is a hint of something beyond. The breeze can mean a tunnel, or it can mean a string of small air pockets, or it can mean an enormous room. You never know until you clear away the rocks and dirt and make an opening big enough to wriggle in and find out.

The three friends spent their weekends together exploring the cliffs in southeastern France. Eliette Brunel Deschamps was born in this region of dazzling white cliffs called the Ardèche and started caving when she was 18. She knew the paths into the gorges from the cliff tops by heart. Jean-Marie Chauvet's family moved to the area when he was five years old. By the time he was 12, he was caving. He and his friends wore World War II army helmets and scrambled down the limestone rock faces. Christian Hillaire first spied the caves from his kayak when he was a child. While paddling around the sharp bends of the Ardèche River, he would search for the black openings that freckled the cliffs above him. Now grown, the three spent their weekends exploring caves and swallow holes just as they had when they were

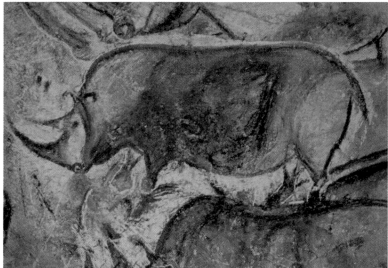

These woolly rhinos painted on the walls of Chauvet Cave became extinct toward the end of the last Ice Age. Some members of this species had horns almost five feet long.

children. Only now Chauvet's helmet was a miner's helmet with a headlamp instead of a World War II model.

That chilly December afternoon, Chauvet, Hillaire, and Deschamps followed an ancient mule path along the ledge until they came to a spot soaked in sun. It warmed them. It was then Chauvet discovered the opening hidden by evergreen oaks. The hole in the side of the cliff was only 30 inches high and 10 inches wide. One at a time the three squeezed through into an opening with a sloping floor and a ceiling just high enough for them to stand up—barely. The slope in the floor led them downward and they let it pull them forward, following the billowing draft. The draft was coming from a hole in the floor. They stretched out on their stomachs, the slope of the floor angling their bodies so that their feet were higher than their heads. The three peered into the black hole. They felt the breeze. Yes, it was there, but the rock was dry... could this simply be a wind that passed through and not the breath of a hidden cave? There was only one way to find out, so they took turns removing stones, enlarging the opening.

The tunnel ran like an air-conditioning duct through a house—straight down, a twist, then straight up again—opening into a room. Only this room was made of rock. Deschamps squiggled in first—headfirst—her headlamp

ART LESSONS

Archaeologists group prehistoric art into two categories. One category is portable art, art that is meant to be carried around. The other category is parietal art, from the Latin word *paries*, meaning "wall." Parietal art is drawn, painted, engraved, or sculpted on large rocks and rock walls such as in caves.

A lot of portable art is gone. Wood, bark, hide, and feather are all perishable. Body painting, song, and dance all disappear with the artists.

Flutes were made from hollowed bird, reindeer or bear bones. One bone with two holes in it is estimated to be 82,000 years old. Could this have been some Neandertal's instrument? Or did some hungry animal just puncture the bone with its teeth?

the only light in the pitch black. She squirmed along with her arms stretched out in front of her until the floor dropped away—three stories away. The beam of her headlamp traveled only so far into the velvety black, then faded away. She let out a hoot and listened for the echo to judge the size of the room. The echo seemed to lose itself in the cave. This room was huge! They would need a ladder to climb down into it.

Their van was at the base of the cliff and they hurried back to get a rope ladder. But it was dark, it was late, and they were tired. Did they want to wait until the next weekend? Something told them no—don't wait. Chauvet felt that prickle at the back of his neck. He forgot that he was tired. It was pitch black in the cave even at high noon, so what did the darkness matter? They climbed back up the mule path, through the narrow opening, down, around, and up the duct. At the edge of the tunnel, they unrolled their ladder. The end of the ladder disappeared into the dark. They could not see the bottom. What were they climbing down into?

Chauvet went first this time. Down, down, down he climbed. He turned his head this way and that as he lowered himself into the black hole, pointing the headlamp's beam in all directions. When he finally reached the floor, the smell of clay was so strong he felt as if he could taste it. The room was so quiet that he could hear his heart pounding in his ears.

Once they had all reached the bottom, they inched forward single file. It looked as if they were playing follow the leader, each person careful to step in the exact footprint of the person in front of him. They didn't want to disturb the floor any more than necessary. The room was too large for their headlamps to light. They couldn't see how deep it ran and could barely make out the

Cave bear bones litter the floor of Chauvet Cave in France. These animals hibernated in the cave and probably died natural deaths.

❝ Cave bear bones, Chauvet Cave, France, 32,000–24,500 years ago

walls alongside them. Chauvet felt something under his foot, just as he was about to put his weight on it. A bone! Now they were even more careful walking through the cavernous room. They didn't want to disturb any bones—and there were hundreds of them scattered across the floor ahead. All over the floor there were round hollows, as if some giant had left thumbprints everywhere. Chauvet realized the indentations were bear hibernation nests. The bones must have once been cave bears.

Deschamps let out a cry. The others jerked their heads to see what it was that had startled her. On the wall, in the beam of her headlamp, they saw the red outline of a mammoth. Prehistoric people had been here.

The three walked carefully forward, one step at a time. They were so stunned that they couldn't speak. All they could manage was one "ah" after another. They pointed, trying to get each other's attention—here, there, no, over here. There was too much to see. They passed paintings of

❝ Cave bear drawing, Chauvet Cave, France, 32,000–24,500 years ago

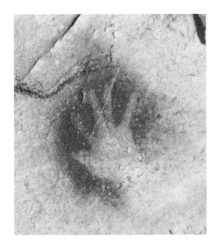

Hand stencil, Chauvet Cave, France, 32,000–24,500 years ago

Fire remains, Chauvet Cave, France, 32,000–24,500 years ago

a red bear, a bird with its wings spread, a rhinoceros with a huge curved horn. The paintings were drawn in red and black and yellows... hundreds of them. They came faster now, a mammoth, a lion, then more rhinoceros... herds of beasts overlapping, leaping, seeming to reach out to them from the walls. Chauvet writes in his book *Dawn of Art,* "Suddenly we felt like intruders. Deeply impressed, we were weighed down by the feeling that we were not alone; the artists' souls and spirits surrounded us. We thought we could feel their presence; we were disturbing them."

They passed one painting after another, each more amazing than the last... there, look! Handprints. There, look! Symbols... what do they mean? The paintings were so vivid that they felt that with the next turn, they would come upon the artists—Cro-Magnon wearing animal skins and holding a stick of charcoal. Chauvet recalls, "As we always do, we kept our distance and made no attempt to approach the painted wall in order to preserve any prints that the prehistoric people might have left at its foot."

Their headlamps dimmed as the battery power grew low. They knew they had to go back before they lost all light. Walking back, in their fading beams, they saw drawings of hyena, panther, ibex, and bears... some so high the artist must have climbed up on something to draw them.

Once they had collected lighting equipment and video cameras, they returned to the cave. This time they noticed the walls were smudged with black smears where torches had been scraped against the rock. Did the torches light the gallery for the artist? Or did the artist build a fire on the floor? Chauvet could imagine the beasts lit by dancing flames. They would look as if they were moving. Deschamps pointed to a spot on the floor where a fire had been lit 32,000 years ago. There was no evidence of cooked bones anywhere. The fire had been for light, not for cooking. In fact, there was no rubbish of the type that comes with early human living places.

No one had ever lived in this cave—except the bears. Claw marks grooved the rock. There must have been hundreds of bears that had lived in the cave. They had lived here

for thousands of years before and after the artists, stretching and sharpening their claws on the walls. One prehistoric artist took advantage of the claw marks and engraved a horse, incorporating the bear's scratches into the carving. On a block that had fallen from the ceiling, someone had placed a bear skull. It still looked ferocious even though it had been dead for tens of thousands of years. Had this skull been placed on the block for a ceremony? Or was the artist's young child just entertaining herself while waiting patiently for her parent to finish painting?

Cave art must have been important to prehistoric people. The caves weren't pleasant artists' studios in which to work. They were usually pitch black, cold, and damp. Why did ancient artists feel the need to paint there? Caves are dramatic places. Could prehistoric humans have performed rituals in them? Did they use caves as function halls to celebrate children becoming adults? Some scholars think that the artists were shamans—holy men painting in trances, hoping to contact the spirit world. Or maybe the artists were storytellers who drew the history of their people on the walls—leaving a record for those who came after them with torches to light up the past.

A cave bear skull sits just where the artists of Chauvet Cave placed it, on top of a boulder that fell from the cave's ceiling. Charring indicates a fire had been lit on the boulder before the skull was placed there.

Paleos + *lithos* = "old" +
"stone"
The Old Stone Age is the
archaeologist's term for the
period from the first stone
tools to the end of the
last Ice Age

CARBON CLOCKS

The torch marks on the walls of Chauvet Cave were perfect for determining how old the wood was that made the torch. Living things contain carbon 14, which has an atomic clock. When the living thing dies, it is as if a timer begins ticking. The carbon 14 breaks down at a constant rate. About every 5,700 years, half disappears.

In the first 5,700 years, half of the carbon 14 disappears—leaving half behind. Every 5,700 years what is left is cut in half. Around the 40,000 year mark there is no longer enough carbon 14 to measure. Things older than 40,000 years need other dating methods.

There are scholars who think that prehistoric humans believed in hunting magic. The artists painted animals on the walls so that the hunters would have good luck. If an animal was speared on the cave wall, it would later be speared in the hunt. Chauvet Cave threw a hitch into that thinking. Prehistoric humans did not hunt rhinoceros, and yet there they were on the cave walls. Prehistoric art specialist Paul Bahn writes in the introduction to Chauvet's book that "generally, the animals drawn in the **Paleolithic** caves are hunted animals . . . here, the dangerous animals, which did not form part of the Paleolithic menus, constitute the great majority."

The discovery of Chauvet Cave rocked the rock art world. Dating back 32,000 years, it was the oldest cave art known. There are animals that make their first appearance in Chauvet Cave—the owl, the panther, and the hyena. The skill of the artists is also amazing. The artists captured their subject through shading and angle. The drawings *still* raise the hair on the back of Chauvet's neck. And the three friends *still* spend every free moment cave-diving in the Ardèche.

Archaeologist Jean Clottes takes notes while kneeling beside images of horses. He crouches carefully so as not to disturb anything on the floor of the cave.

CHAPTER 17

DOUBTING THOMAS
PEOPLING OF THE AMERICAS

❝ ANIMAL AND PLANT REMAINS, TOOL, AND STRUCTURES IN CHILE

Archaeology is a lot like life. Just when you think you have all the answers someone comes along and changes the questions. Archaeologist Thomas Dillehay changed the questions. He probably didn't want to. No one likes the guy who digs up evidence that suggests everyone has been wrong all these years. Scholars try to bully you because they don't believe you—they don't *want* to believe you. Of course scholars don't bully by physically pushing (at least most of the time). They bully by asking pointed questions. So Dillehay, could the wind have blown the trees down in just the right pattern so it looked like a shelter? And Dillehay, couldn't that mastodon, which you claim was butchered, have felt sick and eaten those stones, dropped dead, and then sometime later humans made a shelter near his carcass and cut at his bones? (Scholars really asked these questions—they were desperate to prove Dillehay wrong.)

It appeared that everyone was doubting Thomas Dillehay. At times he must have wished that he had never seen that

SHAGGY BEASTS

Elephants may look a lot like mastodons, but they are not their descendants. Just as humans and apes parted from a common ancestor millions of years ago and are just cousins, so it goes with elephants and mastodons. They went their separate ways more than 20 million years ago.

Mastodons and mammoths may look alike, but they had many differences. The biggest difference was their teeth. Mammoths' teeth were designed for grinding grasses. The mastodon's teeth were more rounded for eating softer plants found in swampy areas. Sometime around 10,000 years ago they died out, along with many other large mammals in the Americas. Climate changes made it hard for them to find enough food. Some scholars believe overhunting contributed to their death sentence.

What's that smell? The mastodon investigates in this artist's reconstruction. The mastodon looks like a furry elephant, only slightly shorter and stockier with upward curving tusks.

" Mastodon bone, Monte Verde, Chile, 12,500 years ago

" Stone drill, Monte Verde, Chile, 12,500 years ago

mastodon bone—or at least that it hadn't turned out to be so old. But he did see the bone, and it did turn out to be that old, so there was no turning back. . . .

In the 1970s, near the southernmost tip of South America, in Monte Verde, Chile, a father and son were chopping back the brush alongside a small creek to make way for their ox carts. Squishing through the wet bog they noticed the bones of an extinct animal—bones that they found from time to time on their land. When they looked closer they noticed stone tools—tools that looked as ancient as the bones.

When Thomas Dillehay first saw the mastodon bones, he was curious about the mysterious markings on them. Were the marks made by animals tromping over the bones? *Or* could humans have scored them with stone tools? From looking at the site where the bones were found, Dillehay assumed that the marks were made by Ice-Age settlers. When the carbon dating test results came in, and he learned that the settlement was more than 12,000 years old, he thought that there must have been a mistake. Those dates

This stream cuts through part of the archaeological site at Monte Verde.

were not possible. Dillehay's team took more tests. The dates were accurate.

How could this be? For years the accepted theory was that the first humans in the Americas were people called the Clovis. They were big-game hunters who had followed herds of mammoth out of Siberia. But Monte Verde in Chile, all the way down near the tip of South America, was older by a thousand years than the oldest Clovis sites. If the Clovis people weren't the first Americans, as scholars had thought, who were? And where did they come from?

Up until the time of the Monte Verde discovery, scholars had assigned the first Americans a tidy itinerary for their entry into the continent. The problem was that *that* route made the settlement at Monte Verde impossible. The accepted theory claimed that the first Americans arrived during the last ice age, when the Bering Sea had dried up to expose a broad plain between Siberia and Alaska—the Bering Land Bridge. If they did come that way, the *when* was critical. Not only did they have to hit the Bering Land Bridge at the right time, when sea levels were low enough, but there was also another formidable obstacle ahead of them—ice—and lots of it.

Two glaciers blocked their path—at least most of the time. Occasionally, when the earth warmed up enough, a crack opened between the two ice sheets. The mile-wide corridor was likely to have been wet and muddy from the melting ice. That must have been hard going for our Siberian immigrants.

Between about 20,000 and 14,000 years ago, there was no ice-free corridor. The crack between glaciers was closed. Did the Monte Verde people come *before* that entrance slammed shut? Or did they enter the Americas another way? What if walking wasn't the only migration route? What if prehistoric humans also floated down the Pacific coast in boats?

Well, you can imagine, *that* got the scholars all worked up. The "Clovis First" theory was like a favorite child. No one wanted to give it up. The Clovis people were noble hunters. They were the kind of ancestors you could brag

---

AMERICAN ARRIVALS

60,000–10,000 years ago
Bering Land Bridge was exposed, allowing people to cross from Siberia to North America

20,000 years ago
People *may* have camped in Meadow-croft Rockshelter, Pennsylvania

12,500 years ago
People settled at Monte Verde, Chile

11,200 to 10,900 years ago
Clovis people hunted mammoth and other animals in North America

8,400 years ago
Kennewick Man buried beside the Columbia River in Washington

MEANWHILE IN THE NORTH-WESTERN USA...

In July 1996 two students stumbled onto a skull stuck in the Columbia riverbank, in Kennewick, Washington. Because of the shape of the skull and the homestead trash nearby, people thought the skeleton must have been that of a pioneer.

At the morgue the forensic anthropologist began his routine observations on the remains: Adult male, five feet nine inches tall, medium build, about 45 years old at the time of death... when suddenly the routine observations turned into anything *but* routine. He noticed something stuck in the hip bone—a spear point—a *stone* spear point. And it looked like it was thousands of years old. Who *was* this man? Just how long ago did he die? He's now known as Kennewick Man, and he died more than 8,400 years ago.

about. They hunted the Columbian mammoth. This fearsome tusked beast could stand 13 feet high at the shoulder and weigh 9 tons. The Clovis people designed a special spear point to do the job. Flaked from stone to razor sharpness, the long point sank deeper with each step the mammoth took. Every movement added to the beast's blood loss, until it weakened and fell. Clovis points are so beautifully made that they are considered works of art. Scholars have admired these people ever since they first found the bones of a mammoth that had been riddled with the points in Clovis, New Mexico. This was the stuff legends are made from. Who would want to let that story of noble hunters go?

Monte Verde created chaos for the "Clovis First" theory. Thomas Dillehay writes in *The Settlement of the Americas* that "humans were in the Americas much earlier than we previously thought and that for much of that time the first Americans were not just big-game hunters but plant-food gatherers as well." It was also becoming clear to Dillehay that describing the first Americans as *one* group of people was most likely wrong. He writes, "first immigrants probably came from several different places in the Old World and...

Excavations in progress at Monte Verde, Chile. Plastic sheets keep the deposits that have not yet been excavated dry.

their genetic heritage and physical appearance were much more diverse than we thought."

Thomas Dillehay knew that Monte Verde would get the scientific community riled up. He knew that other scientists would try to discredit him. They would claim that his research was sloppy. They would claim that he made mistakes when he dated the site. They would claim that he misinterpreted the clues. But that didn't stop him. He wrote, "Here was an intriguing mystery. Over the next ten years, I directed a research team of more than eighty professionals." His team dug up "wooden, bone and stone tools, as well as scraps of animal hide and chunks of meat, human footprints, hearths, and thousands of edible and medicinal plants." All of which they found centering around the "remains of wooden hut foundations in Monte Verde." Things that normally would have rotted or dried up and turned to dust were preserved by partially decayed plant matter called peat, which coated the artifacts and protected them inside an airtight seal.

Opportunities to study open-air settlements don't occur very often. Exposure to the elements over time destroys them. Monte Verde gave scientists a chance to see what kind of structures people built thousands of years ago. Dillehay writes about one of the structures: "a 20-

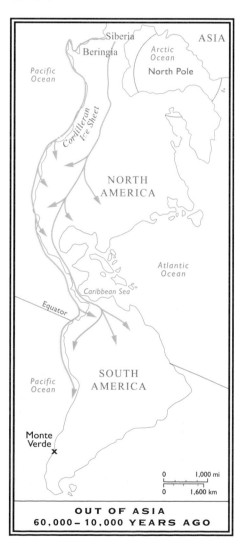

OUT OF ASIA
60,000 – 10,000 YEARS AGO

The arrows indicate possible routes that humans took entering the Americas from Asia. The Cordilleran Ice Sheet covered the Rocky Mountains during the last Ice Age. Beringia is the name of the land bridge connecting Siberia to Alaska during periods of lower sea levels during the last Ice Age.

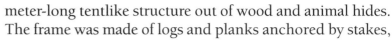

Structure, Monte Verde,
Chile, 12,500 years ago

meter-long tentlike structure out of wood and animal hides. The frame was made of logs and planks anchored by stakes, and the walls were poles covered with animal hides." Like a detective, Dillehay reconstructs the interior of the structure from the clues he finds. "The tent's dirt floor is embedded with hundreds of microscopic flecks of hide tissue, suggesting that it was probably covered with animal skins. Inside the tent, individual living spaces were divided by planks and poles."

The people at Monte Verde cooked in clay-lined pits in their individual rooms inside the tent. But they also cooked as a community in one of the two large hearths outside.

Dillehay describes a second structure as wishbone-shaped. The foundation was made by mixing sand with

Foundation, Monte Verde,
Chile, 12,500 years ago

The base of this small building or shelter was discovered by Thomas Dillehay in excavations at Monte Verde.

animal fat, and then wooden posts were set into the cement-like mixture. This was a place where people made tools, butchered mastodon, and prepared hides—a place to gather and work together.

Thomas Dillehay believes this structure was also a hospital of sorts. He found evidence of plants that are used to treat skin and lung problems. Half the medicinal plants grew near Monte Verde, but there were many that grew only on the coast more than 40 miles away, and one from the north that came an astounding distance of more than 400 miles. The people who lived at Monte Verde either traveled long distances or traded with people who lived far away—or both.

66 Plant remains, Monte Verde, Chile, 12,500 years ago

Each family at Monte Verde had a special job to perform. Some collected plants from the coast; others hunted animals in the nearby forest. Scientists are surprised at how complex social life was at Monte Verde. It was time to let go of the story that *all* Ice-Age people were big-game hunters following mammoth. Monte Verde shows us ice age people living year-round in one place, gathering plants and hunting small game.

Every so often scientists discover a site that changes the theories. Monte Verde is one. Scientists now accept Monte Verde to be as old as the tests say. They now know the route into the Americas is not as simple and direct as they once thought. Some things haven't changed. The first Americans did cross that Bering Land Bridge that connected Siberia to Alaska. They did come out of Asia. But from there the story takes as many turns as our ancestors must have. As Thomas Dillehay wrote, "My hunch is that people were coming into the Americas by different routes at different times, and that once better geological evidence is available, we will see that both coastal and interior routes were used, and more than once."

No one is doubting Thomas anymore.

MEANWHILE IN THE EASTERN USA...

To complicate matters, a site in the eastern United States—Meadowcroft Rockshelter in Pennsylvania—may be older than both Clovis and Monte Verde. The tools found below the Clovis layer at Meadowcroft were similar to tools found in Siberia 24,000 years ago.

CHAPTER 18

EARTH'S PHOTO ALBUMS
THE END OF THE LAST ICE AGE

" Plant and animal fossils,
Los Angeles, California,
40,000–10,000 years ago

Beverly Hills probably makes you think of swimming pools and movie stars—not an Ice Age. But if you are looking for a picture of the last Ice Age, there is no better place to go. Near those hills, a few miles from downtown Los Angeles, are the La Brea tar pits. This bubbling crude contains riches more valuable than black gold to researchers trying to re-create what southern California looked like when humans first moved in. From the pits they've pulled giant bones of mammoths and tiny microfossils. There are fossils of mammals and birds and plants and mollusks and insects—hundreds of organisms from the last Ice Age.

The tar pits aren't actually pits. They are puddles—very sticky puddles. Any animal chased into the tar became trapped like a fly stuck to flypaper. Of course, so did the thing doing the chasing. The trapped animals eventually died of shock, dehydration, or starvation. Scavengers attracted by the scent of death, thinking they were onto an easy meal, followed and also became stuck.

The oil coated the victims' bones. This waterproof seal protected them from damage. It preserved the bones along with the pollen that blew in, and the plants that grew nearby, and the insects that landed on the sticky surface when they came to eat the scavenger that came to eat the predator that came to eat the prey. The whole lot is an oily diorama of the prehistoric past.

A workman stands next to mammoth leg bones in Pit 9 at La Brea during excavations in 1914. His own leg looks puny in comparison.

A mastodon is trapped in the La Brea tar pits in this reconstruction. Wolves would have come to feast on the mastodon and then become trapped, too.

STUCK IN TIME

The La Brea tar pits hold snapshots of extinct organisms from birth to death. A single fossil can't show the researcher all the stages of life. The right collection can. La Brea is like a proud parent's photo album. When we flip through it, we see animals in all stages of their lives, just the way the first Americans saw them.

Imagine living 10,000 years ago. Your grandfather followed the herds of shaggy woolly mammoth from Siberia into Alaska. You remember the stories he told of the struggle to survive on the frigid **tundra**. (If your own grandfather tells the old story, "I walked six miles to school in the dead of winter—uphill—both ways," you can relate.) Even though you hunted many things large and small, you identified with one particular beast—for the Clovis people, it was the mammoth. Your grandfather was a mammoth hunter. Your father was a mammoth hunter. And now you are a mammoth hunter. There's only one problem. There are no more mammoth.

You've been eating mammoth for as long as you can remember. What will you eat with those root vegetables now? Bison burgers? That spear you've been using to hunt mammoth is going to need some adjustments if you plan on hunting bison now. Those butchering tools will have to be redesigned, too. Oh, and the houses you made back in

A tundra is one of the vast, nearly level, treeless regions that make up the greater part of the north of Russia, with arctic climate and vegetation. The term also applies to similar regions in Siberia and Alaska.

IT'S THE PITS

Whereas visitors to the La Brea tar pits watch from platforms above, researchers climb down into an excavation pit that is smaller than a sunken version of your classroom. The oil stinks and it clings to everything—clothes, hair, and skin. Excavators suck up gobs of liquid tar with turkey basters, trying to clear out the oil-slicked, black water to find the bones below. They wish it was the Ice Age now. Temperatures would be a few degrees cooler—more like it is in San Francisco than the 90-degree Los Angeles summer heat. You won't hear any complaints though. Nowhere is there a better picture of what prehistoric humans saw when they first stepped out of the ice-free corridor than the one preserved in the pits.

Siberia with mammoth tusks? Forget it. No more woolly mammoth, no more tusks. You're going to have to come up with new building materials.

When a large part of your lifestyle revolves around one of the animals you hunt, and then that animal is taken away, big changes have to be made. The changes can spread through all parts of your life, large and small, from the tusks that provided the roof over your head, to the bone you splintered for a sewing needle. Fortunately, humans are good at adapting to change.

Thousands of years ago there were no forecasts of global warming. No one warned people that their world was about to heat up. They didn't know that the glaciers were about to melt and that when they did, the coasts would flood. If sea levels rose today like they did 10,000 years ago, the sky-scrapers in U.S. coastal cities would need water wings. Boston, New York, Miami, and Los Angeles would all be under water.

You would think that people around the world might enjoy their new climate. After all, an ice age is no day at the beach. But not everything likes balmy temperatures. There are grasses that thrive in cold climates. When it gets warm, they die. The grasslands are replaced by trees. Guess who ate those disappearing grasses? Woolly mammoth. Unlike humans, woolly mammoth aren't known for their adapt-ability. When the mammoth could no longer find the grass-es they were used to eating, their numbers dwindled until there were no more.

It wasn't only the mammoth that died off. Most of the great beasts—the megafauna—that were found in the La Brea tar pits died, too: the sabertooths, the giant ground sloths, the camels, and bears. The idea that the changes caused by the new weather killed them all off is called the "Climate Change Hypothesis." But not everyone buys this explanation. Many scientists don't think that the end was so innocent. There is another theory lurking—murder!

The "Overkill Hypothesis" points a finger at another suspect—the hunter. Hunters swept across the continent armed with spears designed for death. Eleven thousand years ago giant mammals shook the Americas. Ten thousand years ago they were gone. Once the mammoths were gone, the lions and sabertooths that preyed on them died, too—along with the scavengers. Did humans cause the largest mass extinction of large mammals in the history of the planet?

Some scientists believe that the mammoth died out because it was overhunted. Others can't imagine a few humans armed with pointy rocks tied to the end of sticks wiping out an entire species. The question remains: Why did so many species die out in such a short time? Was it the climate change? Or did humans kill too many of them? Or both?

With the large mammals gone, smaller animals moved in. One of those smaller animals—the wolf—befriended humans. Or did it? No one knows who made the first move toward friendship. Was it the human? Or was it the wolf? Did children bring orphaned pups into camp and raise them, taming them from wolves to dogs, only to learn how useful they could be? Wolves, with their keen senses of smell and hearing, must have saved more than one napping human by barking and growling at some deadly beast on the prowl. Or was it the wolf who quickly realized that humans meant dinner and approached camps for leftovers? Curling up by the fire with a mammoth bone has got to be the ultimate dog fantasy.

The first dogs in the Americas appear to have migrated along with the people from Asia across the Bering Land Bridge. Why did humans travel with dogs? They didn't have the luxury of feeding another mouth unless it was very important to them. Did the dogs pull sleds? Did they protect the bands of humans from predators? Did they hunt for "the pack"?

Maybe the wolves followed the humans, scavenging scraps along the way. Although it is unclear why dogs came to the Americas originally, once they were there, it is clear that humans valued them. At

COOL CATS

One of the most common animals found in the tar pits is the sabertooth cat. The remains of thousands of them have been found. Scientists do not call them sabertooth tigers. There is no such thing as a sabertooth tiger! The sabertooth's short tail is one of the characteristics that puts it in the group with cats, not tigers.

 Dog grave, Koster, Illinois, 8,500 years ago

Koster, Illinois, a North American archaeological site, there are graves where dogs have been carefully buried.

When we look at the pictures in the La Brea tar pits photo album, we see the landscape just how the first Americans saw it—fertile and flourishing. When we look at the pictures in the Koster photo album, we see how people lived once they had spread through the New World and had begun to settle down. When the Ice Age ended and the menu changed, some people stayed put, eating what they could find locally. With the big game gone, people began to think smaller—raccoons and rabbits—things they could count on finding. Koster is a good example of how those people lived.

Koster's layers are arranged like a stack of pancakes. Each pancake represents a particular time of human habitation. Some were big and some were small. Over thousands of years the stack grew as settlement after settlement occupied Koster. The stack is rather sloppy, not only because of size, but also because some villages were a little to the west or a little to the east of the one before it. The pancakes are all different thicknesses, too, and in some cases pretty lumpy, depending on how many people lived in one spot and for how long. There are 26 pancakes in the stack.

Each layer is called a horizon. Horizon 11 was occupied nearly 8,500 years ago. It was a tiny village, no more than three quarters of an acre, where about 25 people came every

TEMPERATURES PLUMMET

Temperatures have always gone up and come down. Right now we are between cold snaps. But the glaciers will come again. You may think these climate changes are so slow that you would barely notice. But there are paleoclimatologists— scientists who study ancient climates—who are taking a look at the chemical make-up of air bubbles that were trapped in the ice 13,000 years ago. The paleoclimatologists think the climate change entering the last Ice Age was fast. They think it could have happened in just 10 years.

year during the same season. In the center of the village many fires burned in hearths, some rimmed with limestone. Here the people roasted deer, and while it sizzled and popped, they ground nuts. At Horizon 11's thickest point, there are 18 inches of debris left behind by these Koster people—woodworking tools, sewing tools, even jewelry.

In Horizon 11 we find eastern North America's oldest cemetery. Oval pits were dug for the dead in this special burying place. The bodies were positioned on their sides with their knees tucked into their chests and were left uncovered until they began to rot. A child, one and half years old, had been dusted with red powder. Not far away, the Koster people buried their dogs.

The next pancake—er—occupation is quite different. Horizon 10 was a workplace for toolmakers. They came, they worked, and they went home to eat and sleep.

Bone and clay beads, Koster, Illinois, 8,500 years ago

Each layer in this stack is a different occupation at Koster. The layers span more 8,500 years. Imagine your home 8,500 years from now, at the bottom of a stack similar to this one.

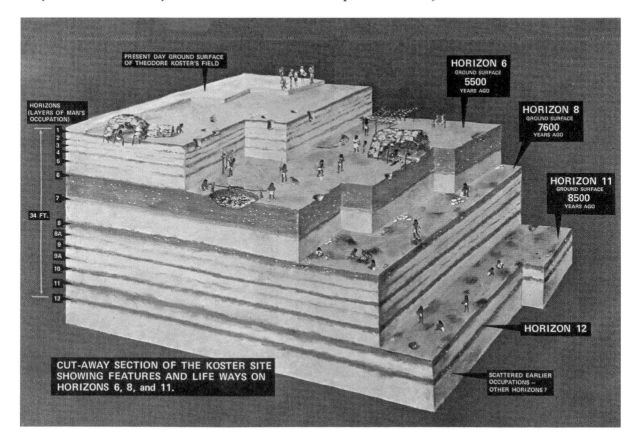

PRESENT DAY GROUND SURFACE OF THEODORE KOSTER'S FIELD

HORIZON 6
GROUND SURFACE
5500
YEARS AGO

HORIZON 8
GROUND SURFACE
7600
YEARS AGO

HORIZON 11
GROUND SURFACE
8500
YEARS AGO

HORIZON 12

HORIZONS
(LAYERS OF MAN'S OCCUPATION)
1
2
3
4
5
6
7
8
8A
9
9A
10
11
12

34 FT.

CUT-AWAY SECTION OF THE KOSTER SITE SHOWING FEATURES AND LIFE WAYS ON HORIZONS 6, 8, and 11.

SCATTERED EARLIER OCCUPATIONS -- OTHER HORIZONS ?

Lifestyles changed again in Horizon 8. Koster settlements 7,600 years ago were built for year-round living. Horizon 8 holds four separate occupations, each lasting 100 years or more. The people who lived there dug out flat areas in the hillside on which to build homes. They toppled trees for construction. Now that the people weren't pulling up camp every season, they put more effort into building their homes.

Once the people built houses, they began to collect things to put in them. By Horizon 6 people had begun collecting things other than the tools they needed for living. In the graves of both men and women, right near their heads, archaeologists have found bone pins shaped like clothespins with engraved handles. They think the pins were for hair. Because these pins have shown up in Indiana, Missouri, and Kentucky, people probably traded them. Imagine trading your barrettes (boys wore them, too). What do you think you could get for one?

Hunter-gatherers don't have much in the way of material things to fight over. But with permanent settlements comes an accumulation of "stuff." Your neighbor may have a nicer ax, but he's eyeing that knife you got in trade for your finest white-tailed deer skin. The fellow down the alleyway has stored more dried meat than he can possibly use. And that woman wearing the fancy beaded necklace is sure full of herself. People were starting to experience envy. Some were gaining importance in the community according to what they had and how much. All the while, the occupation level thickens with the belongings of these people.

⟨⟨ Hairpins, Koster, Illinois, 8,000 years ago

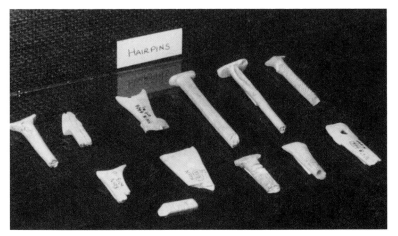

Men and women both used these hair pins to hold their hair up and out of their faces.

CHAPTER 19

THE FARMER IN THE TELL

DOMESTICATION OF PLANTS AND ANIMALS

It was a race against the clock. Syrian engineers were building a dam across the Euphrates River. Soon the **tell** at Abu Hureyra would be under Lake Assad. Clues to what life was like in a 10,000-year-old village soon would disappear into a watery grave. Archaeologists had to recover whatever they could before the dam flooded the area.

They dug trenches—seven of them—some more than two stories deep. They dug on days when it was so hot that the skin on the backs of their necks blistered. They dug on days when it was so cold that they could barely move their frozen fingers. Israel and Syria went to war. And still they dug. The engineers raced to finish building the dam. The scientists raced to finish excavating the tell. They worked through the heat and the cold and the danger.

Why this particular tell? What made it so important? Archaeologists had a question and they hoped the answer was buried at Abu Hureyra. People began living at Abu

{ Tell is an Arabic word that means mound left by human occupation.

People tend camels and sheep in front of Tell Abu Hureyra. Scientists study this mound, or tell, to try to better understand when, why, and how humans stopped hunting and gathering and started farming.

Hureyra when they were hunter-gatherers—when they ate wild plants and hunted wild animals. And they still lived there again after they had turned into farmers—when they tended gardens and herded animals. Why did people change? Could archaeologists find out from the evidence at Abu Hureyra? Could they dig up enough clues before the water washed them all away?

Sherlock Holmes studied dead bodies. The famous fictional detective dazzled readers with his deductions. The murderer must be left handed and shorter than five-foot-five, he would announce after examining the dead body—after all, the skull had been crushed from the left side and slightly below by a blow from behind only a short, left-handed person could make. **Paleopathologists**, detectives who study *ancient* dead bodies, make Sherlock Holmes look like an amateur. From tiny pieces of bone, they can reconstruct whole lifestyles. Here are just a few of *their* dazzling deductions from Abu Hureyra:

paleo + pathos + logia = "ancient" + "suffering" + "study" Paleopathologists solve puzzles from the past by telling us a great deal about ancient life from studying the dead.

The clue: wear on the big toe bones of women

The reasoning: It takes several hours to grind enough flour for one meal. Long hours of kneeling with the toes curled under can cause the deformities paleopathologists were finding.

The deductions: Women spent long hours on their knees grinding grain. Women did most of the food preparation.

The clue: big neck bones

The reasoning: Neck bones grow unusually large when they have to keep the neck from wobbling under heavy loads.

The deduction: Villagers carried grain, game, and building materials in baskets on their heads.

Homo sapiens sapiens toe bones, Abu Hureyra, Syria, 9,000 years ago

Homo sapiens sapiens neck bone, Abu Hureyra, Syria, 9,000 years ago

66 *Homo sapiens sapiens* arm bones, Abu Hureyra, Syria, 9,300 years ago

The clue: bulges in the upper arm bones

The reasoning: Villagers developed big muscles from lifting something heavy over and over, like weight lifters. The bone got bigger to support the bigger muscles.

The deduction: Villagers pounded the grain with mortars and pestles, the first step in turning the tough seeds into flour.

The clue: grooves in the teeth

66 *Homo sapiens sapiens* teeth, Abu Hureyra, Syria, 9,300 years ago

The reasoning: How many times has your mother warned you not to use your teeth as a tool? No one warned the basket weavers at Abu Hureyra. They used their teeth to hold cane, freeing up their hands to weave. After a while the cane wore grooves in their teeth. People with this particular damage to their teeth were only found in one area. Some of the people's teeth found in this area were worn right down to the root. These people also had big jaw joints. Could they have been chewing plant fiber to make string? Paleopathologists think so.

The deductions: Some of the villagers were specialists—basket weavers and string makers. These craftspeople lived in one area of the village.

The clue: pitted eye sockets

The reasoning: Pitting in the eye sockets comes from parasites eating away at the bone. People catch things more easily when they are crammed together. Animals carry parasites.

The deduction: People at Abu Hureyra lived close together and near their animals.

Of course it's not just bones that show us what village life was like at Abu Hureyra. Archaeologists uncovered the houses. From what was left of the mud-brick walls, we get an idea of what the village looked like. The villagers built their homes close to their neighbors' houses, with only a very narrow alleyway between them. Some had small courtyards. Their houses were windowless rectangles with several small rooms. They used mud to plaster their floors black and their walls white. Although they kept the insides of their

The earliest farming villages began in southwest Asia in an area called the Fertile Crescent, which looks like a giant clown's frown. It was home to a wide variety of wild plants and animals, ancestors to the domestic plants and animals found at Abu Hureyra.

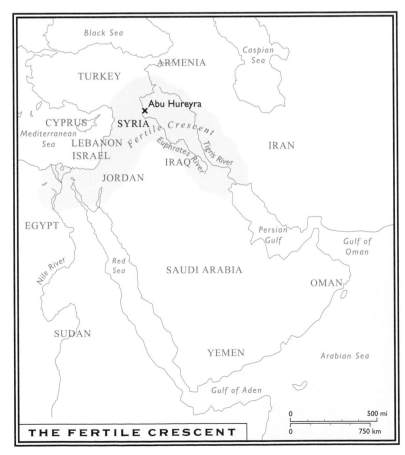

THE FERTILE CRESCENT

homes tidy, the villagers threw their trash out the nearest door and used the alleyways for toilets.

The picture of life at Abu Hureyra was filling in, but there was one puzzle archaeologists were anxious to solve. People had lived at Abu Hureyra for 3,000 years. How long does it take to make a farmer? How do you begin? There were no other farmers to copy. No monthly magazine to tell them which plants made good crops and when to plant. Was the first garden an accident? Did gatherers drop wild seeds along the paths when they brought home plants they had found? Did that give someone the idea to plant seeds?

And why plant at all? It certainly wasn't a better life. Hunter-gatherers have far more free time. Farmers work much harder and many more hours. It wasn't a healthier life. A diet that covers that long list of nutrients in your multivitamin comes from eating many different things. Farmers grew a limited number of things. They ate a limited number of things. They didn't get all the nutrients on that long list. You can have a full belly and still suffer from malnutrition if you don't eat a variety of foods. Hunter-gatherers ate many different plants and animals. They were far more likely than farmers to get close to the recommended daily allowances.

You would think one benefit of farming would be independence. At the very least if you farmed you could count on where your next meal was coming from. Wrong. Just ask any farmer. Whole crops get wiped out in a single storm. Hunter-gatherers just look around for something else to eat.

So why farm? There has to be at least one good reason. Why did agriculture pop up in so many different regions around the world? Did people begin to farm because they had to or because they could? And if they had to farm, what could possibly force them to do it?

Farming does feed more people. It takes 10 square miles of wild land to feed one hunter-gatherer. Farm that same land and you can feed at least 100 people. Were there more people? Scientists who study ancient population sizes have found that when hunter-gatherers began to stay in one place like Abu Hureyra, their numbers grew. The need to

TIPS FOR TAMING

Why did the villagers tame sheep and goats instead of gazelles? Some animals are easier to tame than others. Gazelles panic. If you pen a gazelle, it will kill itself trying to get out. If you want to pick the right animal to tame, here are some helpful hints:

Herbivores are cheaper to feed than carnivores.

Pick an animal that grows quickly.

Make sure it will breed in captivity.

The animal should be easy to handle. A rhinoceros may have lots of meat, but no one would want to get in the pen with it.

Animals that follow a leader, such as herders, are easier to manage and move about.

feed more people was probably one of the major reasons people started farming.

Of course, once they completely gave up traveling their numbers increased even more. If you are on the move, you need to carry your children from place to place until they can keep up. Having a child about once every four years is all a woman in a wandering band could handle. Farmers, however, could have children every two years.

The more people clump together, the more problems develop—especially when people dump human waste just outside the door. Disease spreads. With all the problems that crop up with farming, it makes you wonder why hunter-gatherers gave up the good life. Of course, they couldn't know what problems lay ahead, because no one had farmed before. They were just doing the best they could at the time to keep everybody fed.

Farming isn't only about taming wild plants. It's about taming wild animals, too. At Abu Hureyra the villagers began by hunting gazelles. The hunters chased the gazelles into an area surrounded by boulders. Once trapped, the gazelles were easier to kill. Archaeologists aren't sure whether the villagers killed off most of the gazelles or not. What they are sure of is that bones from gazelles were disappearing from village hearths, and in their place they were finding bones from sheep and goats.

Sheep, goats, pigs, cattle, wheat, and barley all existed in the wild around Abu Hureyra. Now they were being raised in the hands of humans. What nature once directed, now humans controlled. People decided which plant flourished, what animal multiplied. Changes were encouraged, as the English naturalist Charles Darwin pointed out in the first chapter of his *Origin of Species,* "not indeed to the animal's or plant's own good, but to man's use or fancy."

Abu Hureyra lies under Lake Assad now, but for years to come scientists will be studying what the archaeologists managed to save before the dam was complete—and making dazzling deductions about the life of the farmer in the tell.

CHAPTER 20

DEAR DIARY
ORIGINS OF SETTLED LIFE

Imagine a wheat field stretching to the horizon like a sea of golden grass. Now imagine a bump in the middle of the wheat field. Most of us would think "hill." But if you're an archaeologist you think "mound." And if you are an archaeologist digging in Turkey you think *"höyük,"* because *höyük* means mound in Turkish. That's exactly what archaeologist James Mellaart thought one cold November evening in 1958 when he sent a worker scrambling 65 feet up to the top of the mound. The sun was setting, but even in the dim light they could make out chunks of mud-brick walls sticking out of the mound at odd angles and stone tools scattered everywhere. Mellaart scraped away dirt with his trowel and discovered white plaster coating the brick walls. "Right from the start I knew that not only was Çatal Hüyük old, but its occupation had lasted a long time," Mellaart told interviewers later.

Mellaart may have known from the start that Çatalhöyük was important, but it was not until he began excavating that he realized he had discovered one of the largest towns on Earth 9,000 years ago—a town that housed as many as 10,000 people in its back-to-back dwellings. The town was packed together so tightly that there was no room for streets. The dwellings were crammed so snugly that doorways had to be cut into the roofs and people had to climb down ladders to enter their homes. Çatalhöyük was a very crowded place.

❝ Flint dagger, Çatalhöyük, Turkey, 9,300–8,100 years ago

NOT A GOOD CHOICE FOR SPELLING BEES

Çatalhöyük is spelled various ways. The current favored spelling seems to be Çatalhöyük, pronounced CHAH-tahl-HU-yook.

A museum exhibit in Ankara, Turkey, gives an idea of what a room at Çatalhöyük may have looked like. Clay cattle heads adorn the walls, and benches are built into the floor.

When Mellaart dug a slice out of the town he found 12 levels of buildings, one on top of the other, spanning nearly 1,500 years. In one section he dug up 200 houses each about the size of your classroom. The houses had built-in furniture—benches, sleeping platforms, and cupboards. The ovens and grain bins were built-in, too. All the surfaces were coated with white plaster. The walls had been painted again and again to refresh them after they had turned sooty from cooking fires. Some houses had been painted 100 times. And on the fresh white surface, artists drew murals.

66 Houses, Çatalhöyük, Turkey, 9,300–8,100 years ago

Mellaart loved to make up stories that could have inspired the murals. One of his favorites was the story he designed to go

⟦66⟧ Mural, Çatalhöyük, Turkey, 9,300–8,100 years ago

This wall painting uncovered at Çatalhöyük, Turkey, dates to somewhere between 8,100 and 9,300 years ago. Some scientists think this painting shows the houses of Çatalhöyük and a nearby volcano in the background.

with a volcano drawing. He believed Çatalhöyük had been the center of trade for the translucent black glass made by volcanoes—obsidian—a material perfect for flaking into razor-sharp edges. The artist, he said, was paying tribute to the source of the town's wealth by painting the volcano where the town's people got the materials to make their tools and their polished black mirrors.

Some houses were more elaborately decorated than others. Some had bull's horns sticking out of the plaster. In others figures were sculpted right into the walls. Each generation added its personal touch until finally the house was torn down and another house built right over the ruins—adding another layer to the mound.

Mellaart has retired now, and Çatalhöyük is in the capable hands of archaeologist Ian Hodder. Where Mellaart scooped artifacts from the soil with his bare hands in the 1960s, Hodder sifts the dirt looking for the bits and pieces of the puzzle today. After the dirt is sifted, it is thrown into barrels of water. Slivers of obsidian sink to the bottom of the barrel, seeds float, and more pieces to the puzzle are separated from the soil. Once the scientists have passed the dirt through the sieves and the water barrels, they examine the mud that is left under a microscope. Hodder tries not to let anything escape his team. Sometimes diggers work for a month in one corner of one house. It is a different time for archaeology. As Mellaart said of the 1960s, "We dug a large

MEANWHILE ALL OVER THE WORLD...

Permanent settlements were springing up in the Near East, China, and the Americas. The oldest known village to date is a 10,500-year-old settlement outside present-day Jericho, in the Middle East. Thousands of years would pass, however, before the first undisputed cities would rise, such as the 5,500-year-old city of Uruk in Mesopotamia.

MEANWHILE IN EURASIA...

When the Ice Age ended and ocean levels rose, the Mediterranean Sea over-flowed and burst through a land barrier that separated it from Lake Euxine 7,600 years ago. Saltwater poured into the freshwater lake. The salt killed millions of fish. The water destroyed farmland and villages.

We think of a dam bursting as a single "whoosh" event, but this flooding lasted many life-times. The water advanced at a steady pace—not so fast that villagers couldn't out run it, but fast enough that their homes were covered in a single day. The water kept coming for 100 years. When it was over, Lake Euxine had become the Black Sea.

66 *Homo sapiens sapiens* skeleton, Çatalhöyük, Turkey, 9,300–8,100 years ago

hole and got out things." Hodder hopes his approach will provide a deeper picture of life at Çatalhöyük.

Hodder encourages his team to talk—talk in the trench-es, talk in the dig house, and talk in their diaries. He hopes that all that talking will help solve the mystery of the ori-gins of settled life. Here's what they were talking about in their diaries in the spring of 1999:

The first few days on site were spent...understand-ing...the layout of an individual house within its one space and relation to others.

Çatalhöyük was rebuilt at least 12 times over its 1,000-year heyday. Houses crumbled and populations swelled. As in any large town, construction was ongoing. Preserving the details of the walls can be a challenge for excavators. Mud brick dries out and quickly erodes when it is exposed to the air. To hold in the moisture, workers spread plastic sheets over the walls, then record the position of each brick. Modern archaeological methods place importance on the site as a whole. It's not just what you dig up, but where it was found in relation to everything else around it. Hodder's team continues in their diaries:

The skull of the skeleton was discovered with the cold steel of a mattock blade and was therefore recovered in a number of pieces... cleaning of the skeleton... revealed the burial to have been of a very young baby....

The cold steel once again located another burial. As I write the skeleton is still being removed.

Under the plaster floors and built-in beds, excavators found skeletons—hundreds of them. There were infants and young children, adults and old people. The people of Çatalhöyük lived on top of their ancestors, generation after generation buried beneath the floors. Scientists believe one possible explanation for the home burials has to do with claims to ownership. The skeletons of your ancestors are proof that your family has lived there. Initially scientists thought that the bodies had been put out in the open before they were buried so that the vultures could pick the bones clean. Modern studies suggest that the bodies were buried intact. Smoke billowing from the open fires in the houses must have helped cover the stink of rotting flesh.

One reason it is exciting to find the bones of the people of Çatalhöyük is that scientists need to know what the residents did for a living. Their jobs define Çatalhöyük. Many scientists don't believe that Çatalhöyük was a city, or even a town. They call it an overgrown village. The difference between a city and a village isn't just about how many people live there or how close together their houses are built, but about what the residents do to support themselves. A "town" is born when some people can eat, not by growing their own food but by trading a skill for food with those who do farm. Townspeople can specialize—in art, in building, in weaving—and still feed their family.

What did the people who lived in Çatalhöyük do? Hodder's team is not finding evidence for specialization.

Several human burials are exposed under a house floor at Çatalhöyük. The black-and-white poles are scales to help the viewer understand how big things really are. Each block of color on a pole is 10 centimeters, or about 4 inches, long.

66 Bricks, Çatalhöyük, Turkey, 9,300–8,100 years ago

The houses are similar to one another, but it looks as if everyone built their own. There is no evidence that there were people supporting themselves as builders. The mud bricks are mixed in almost as many different ways as there are houses. If a professional builder did the mixing you would expect to see the mud brick always made the same way. There are many beautifully crafted objects from obsidian, but it looks as if the people of Çatalhöyük were crafting them in their houses. There is no evidence of people supporting themselves as artists. Instead of finding concentrations of flakes in a few workshops, the flakes are littered around nearly every hearth. Hodder says, "It is hard to imagine 10,000 people, minimally 2,000 families, were going out and doing their own thing, but that is what we see." So *is* Çatalhöyük one of the first cities? Hodder says, "Let's not try to categorize it, as a city or a village, but first try to find out how it works."

66 Obsidian, Çatalhöyük Turkey, 9,300–8,100 years ago

In the diaries of Hodder's team, we see what they see. Perhaps one day they will solve the mysteries of how Çatalhöyük worked, what brought so many people together, and what kept them together. Somewhere in the bits of bones and slivers of stone and clumps of clay, they'll piece together the puzzle of the origins of settled life.

CHAPTER 21

DEAD MEN TALKING
METALS AND MONUMENTS IN EUROPE

For someone who has been dead for more than 5,000 years, the Iceman has a lot to say. He's the best preserved corpse of an ancient man found yet. Most bodies that old have deteriorated until they're nothing more than bits of bones—but not the Iceman, even his eyeballs still remain.

Two hikers found the Iceman in the Italian Alps in the fall of 1991. A melting glacier had revealed the top half of his body. At first everyone thought he was a skier who got caught in a blizzard. Hundreds of people have accidents in the Alps every year. A policeman hacked the Iceman out of the glacier with an ice pick and ski poles he borrowed from passing hikers. He noticed an ax lying nearby that looked primitive, but didn't make much of it. What finally tipped him off to the fact he was dealing with an ancient body was

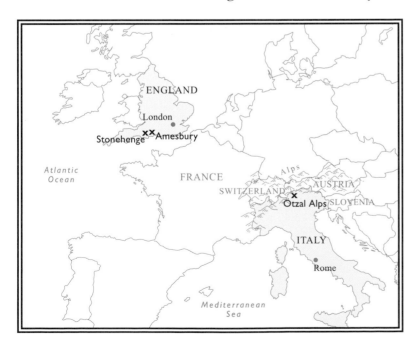

EASY DOES(N'T) IT

Now that the world knew the Iceman was ancient, the way that he was removed from the glacier seems almost barbaric. His ribs may have been cracked when he was pried out of the ice. The jack-hammer used to break up the ice slipped several times and tore through the corpse. It severed the Iceman's dried flesh to the bone around his left hip, buttock, and thigh. The frozen brain shattered from repeated blows to his head against the ice as people tried to yank him free. And his upper left arm snapped in two when he was forced into a wooden coffin. Not only do scientists grieve over the damage done to the Iceman's body, but also over the lost information that could have been obtained through careful excavation.

❝ *Homo sapiens sapiens* remains, Ötzal Alps, Italy, 5,300 years ago

Ötzi's body is kept in cold storage in a museum in Italy at a temperature of about 20 degrees Fahrenheit to prevent further decay.

the flesh. Fresh corpses exposed to the elements have a milky appearance. Fat in the skin mixes with moisture in the air and turns soapy. But the Iceman's skin wasn't white. It was brown and leathery—like an overcooked turkey.

Why was this body so well preserved? Why hadn't it been attacked by flies, foxes, and bears that lived in the mountains? Why didn't the weight of the glacier crush the Iceman? He must have been protected from predators by a snowstorm shortly after he died. He lay facedown in a gully between two ridges. The ridges held the glacier away from him. There he remained in a deep freeze until a freak melt and a pair of hikers delivered him into the hands of scientists.

The Iceman is known as Ötzi (rhymes with "tootsie"), after the Ötzal Alps where he was found. Ötzi had been shot in the back. A flint arrowhead shattered his left shoulder blade, paralyzing his left arm. He died from the wound. Was he a shepherd murdered for his flock? A trader killed for his wares? While some scientists struggle with the questions about his death, others work on Ötzi for information about his life. They wonder if Ötzi can tell them what life was like for Europeans 5,300 years ago.

First scientists wanted to know where Ötzi grew up. They looked at the minerals in his tooth enamel. Food contains minerals from the water and soil where it is grown. As teeth develop they use these minerals for building blocks. Scientists compared the mineral content in Ötzi's teeth to soil in different areas to pinpoint where he spent his childhood.

They determined that he spent his childhood just south of where he was found and his adult life 37 miles north of where he was found.

Then scientists asked Ötzi what people ate in Europe 5,300 years ago. Ötzi's colon answered. It contained wild goat, barley, and cereal. His last supper was red deer and more grain. They found evidence of cooked bread made from wheat—not wild wheat, farmed wheat. Europe had begun farming. They also found pollen in his colon that he must have swallowed in the spring—and that came from plants in Italy. Ötzi had died in the spring on his way out of Italy.

Although Ötzi's colon told scientists that people were farming in Europe, it didn't tell how farming *got* to Europe. Did people like Ötzi bring seeds and cows from fertile farmlands? Or did the northerners hear rumors about other people farming and experiment on their own? Don't even get those scientists started on why. Some argue that climate change was pressuring the Europeans to get busy farming so there would be food on hand. Others argue that there were so few people in Europe that what grew wild was plenty. So why did they begin to farm? Ötzi's colon isn't saying.

Could Ötzi tell scientists how healthy Europeans were 5,300 years ago? Ötzi had arthritis and hardening of the arteries. He'd suffered from a stroke—and recovered. His lungs were black from hearth smoke. His intestines were loaded with parasites that he'd caught from animals. He had fleas. But he didn't have any tooth decay!

Not only had Ötzi avoided rotting; all his stuff had been spared, too. Things that rarely survive thousands of years were found with him—clothing, a wooden ax handle, arrows. Scientists figured that people in Europe had to have worn clothing to keep warm. They just didn't know what the clothes looked like. Now Ötzi's things would show them. His shoes were made from leather and plant fiber and stuffed with grass for warmth. They kept his feet warm and dry. His leggings were made from animal skins. In fact, most of his clothing was made from animal skins. If Europeans were weaving cloth, Ötzi isn't telling.

PEAPODS AND FAMILY PORTRAITS

Plants have family trees, too. Crop evolution can be tracked through the plant's DNA. Scientists begin by collecting DNA from the plant's wild ancestor and then follow the DNA changes created by farming.

Bearskin cap, Ötzal Alps, Italy, 5,300 years ago

Two of his arrows still had feathers. They were attached in such a way to make the arrow spin. Ötzi must have known that if an arrow spins, it will fly true. It won't tip up. It won't tip down. It will fly straight. Ötzi understood physics!

This is all that remains of the Amesbury Archer, who was buried 4,300 years ago along with his possessions.

66 *Homo sapiens sapiens* remains, Amesbury, England, 4,300 years ago

66 Copper knives, Amesbury, England, 4,300 years ago

He also carried fire around with him—embers wrapped in maple leaves, tucked into a birch-bark container. But the item Ötzi carried with him that is most curious was his ax. What was a Stone Age European doing with a copper ax? Not many people had started making things out of metal yet. That started in the Bronze Age. It was still the Stone Age—wasn't it?

In May 2002 archaeologists in Britain found the remains of a man who *was* from the early Bronze Age, about 4,300 years ago. In his grave were things made from metal to prove it. Buried with him were one hundred items, including three copper knives and a pair of gold earrings. The archery equipment from which he got his name includes 16 stone arrowheads and a slate wrist guard. The Amesbury Archer picks up the story where the Iceman left off.

The Archer's tooth enamel shows that he grew up in the Alps—the Iceman's part of the world—not in Britain where he was buried. They both died when they were about the same age—around 40 years old. And they both suffered. The Archer appears to have had an accident a few years before he died that ripped his left kneecap off. The injury would have made the Archer walk with a stiff leg that he had to swing out to the side. He had an abscess on his jaw and a bone infection. He was in constant pain.

The Archer didn't die alone in the mountains like the Iceman. He was buried. And he was buried elaborately. It seems as if all the items placed in his grave were for him to use in the afterlife. He had everything he might need—clothes, tools, weapons, and pots. It looks as if the Archer was a rich and powerful man. In our world rich and powerful is not something new. But for early humankind it was. Throughout most of the Stone Age, humans owned only the basics. They were buried in groups. Someone mourning their death might sprinkle them with red paint, but rich burials were not common because rich lives weren't either.

As the Stone Age came to an end, and trading things caught on, society changed. "Rich" and "poor" now had meaning. Some scientists believe it was the desire for luxuries—such as amber, copper, and gold—that pushed farming into Europe. People needed something to trade for that nicely polished flint ax. That something could be food.

Both the Iceman and the Archer have second names that link them to where their bodies were found. The Archer's second name is the King of Stonehenge. A henge is an enclosure used for ceremonies. Stonehenge, near the village of Amesbury where the Archer was found, is without a doubt the most famous henge, but not the only one by a long shot. Henges appear all over the British Isles, France, and Ireland. There are henges so small you can barely do more than lie down in them, and there is a henge so large that it encircles an entire village.

Clearly the henges were important. No one puts in that kind of effort, lugging 20-ton stones more than 100 miles, without a good reason. Some archaeologists believe that the henges began as cattle enclosures. At a henge centuries older than Stonehenge, archaeologists found the remains of a fence and gate. Could this henge have held cattle? Some

> **BRONZE AGE**
>
> **5,300 years ago**
> Ötzi the Iceman killed in the Alps
>
> **About 5,000–3,500 years ago**
> Stonehenge built and used in England
>
> **4,300 years ago**
> Beginning of the Bronze Age in Europe; Amesbury Archer buried near Stonehenge, England

The giant stones at Stonehenge come from 20 miles away. Scientists debate how they were transported to this spot in what is now Wiltshire, England. As each of these stones weighs more than 25 tons, it was no easy task!

[66] Stonehenge, Wiltshire, England, 4,300 years ago

mega + *lith* = "large" + "stone" Megaliths are the large stones that form prehistoric monuments.

henges were aligned on the midsummer sunrise or the midwinter sunset. The stones were lined up to point to the spot on the horizon where the sun would rise or set. The coming of the growing season, the time of the harvest, the winter rest, would all have great importance to a farmer.

Before Stonehenge was the **megalith** we know today, it was nothing more than a circular bank and ditch. It wasn't until the Archer's time, hundreds of years after it was first built, that the stones were moved in. Archaeologists suspect that the Archer was connected somehow to Stonehenge. The time is right. The location is right. The Archer was buried just three miles from the monument. And it appears from his grave goods that he was a rich and powerful person— important enough to direct the project. Or maybe the Archer was just visiting—drawn to the area by the spiritual pull of Stonehenge. We know he was a traveler. His tooth enamel places him in the Alps; the copper in his knives came from Spain and France. Some things we'll never know. The Iceman and the Archer have their secrets. They're not blabbermouths, after all.

CHAPTER 22

GOT MILK?
FARMING IN AFRICA

Just to prove there is a club out there for *everyone,* consider the club for archaeologists—the Prehistoric Society. And get this—their newsletter is called *Past.* The November 2002 issue of *Past* describes a field trip deep into the Sahara Desert to study how the people who lived there changed from foragers to farmers.

The group of club members climbed into five beat-up SUVs loaded with camping gear and set out into the sea of sand. They soon learned that driving across the desert wasn't the smooth ride you might expect. Graeme Barker, then president of the Prehistoric Society, writes in the newsletter that the only way to approach sand dunes was to "charge full tilt." Otherwise, before reaching the crest of the dune, the SUVs would slide back down. The trick, though, was not to drive so fast that you couldn't stop at the top of the dune, because there was no way of telling as you fishtailed up one side if the other side dropped off like a cliff.

The Sahara Desert sprawls across northern Africa. Today we think of the Sahara as a waterless death trap with nothing but shifting sand dunes. But 7,000 years ago the Sahara was quite different. Then it was grassland spotted with lakes and marshes. The Prehistoric Society's field trip included stops at places that were

"So now where are we?" Members of the archaeologists' club called the Prehistoric Society take a rest at the top of a dune in the Sahara Desert in Libya.

MEANWHILE IN SOUTHEAST ASIA...

More than 2,000 years ago, crops and animals from Southeast Asia began to trickle into Africa. Bananas and chickens were particularly popular. Rice and coconuts were a hit on the east coast.

once lakes. Long ago, lakeside settlements were places for foragers beginning a new way of life. While foraging, these people began to herd animals along the way—moving sheep, cattle, and goats from one grazing land to another.

The Prehistoric Society's first night in the desert was just what you would expect for a bunch of scholars. They'd been delayed because the kitchen truck kept getting flat tires—business as usual when driving in the desert. It was after dark when their drivers found a good spot to set up camp, out of the wind, in a bowl between dunes. The scholars huddled in the beams of the SUV's headlights, flipping through the instructions for pitching their tents.

Almost nothing dampens archaeologists' enthusiasm when they are in hot pursuit of some good prehistory. So the next morning, nearly rested and ready to set off after rock art, the scholars loaded up the vehicles. First though, they had to find gasoline. Barker wrote, "our desert journey needed all the vehicle tanks full as well as the dozen or so jerry cans we also carried...the word...was that there 'probably was' petrol 100 kilometers further south in Ghat, the last settlement before the Algerian and Niger borders." Fortunately "the word" proved true, and they were able to gas up in Ghat. Then they were off to find where and when those Saharan foragers started farming.

African farmers carry home a harvest of sorghum, a cereal grain domesticated in Africa south of the Sahara.

Traditionally scientists had believed that the shift from foraging to herding spread to the Sahara from the Nile Valley 6,000 years ago. The colonists herded their animals westward, carrying plants and pottery along the way. On this field trip the scholars hoped to get a firsthand look at some of the evidence that was pointing toward another theory—one that credits climate changes rather than colonists for farming. Was it all about weather?

More than 8,000 years ago the people in an area of the Middle East called the Fertile Crescent began to farm. The mild wet winters, warm dry summers, and wild plants with *big* seeds practically drew a picture of farming to those foragers. There was no need for a green thumb there.

As with most good ideas, people spread the word. From the Fertile Crescent, farming found its way east and west. But why not north and south? One possible answer is obvious when you look at a map. Eurasia is short and wide, spreading east-west. Africa and the Americas have a tall north-south posture. Have you ever looked at a seed catalog? Have you noticed that plants are recommended for particular zones? Those zones are drawn east to west where temperatures, daylight, and rainfall are similar. Move north and south and conditions change. A plant thriving in southern Florida may shrivel in the cold northeastern United States. For plants that do survive both extremes, the growing seasons may be reversed—what the Montana farmer plants in the spring, the Texan plants in the fall.

As long as farming techniques spread east and west, crops, tools, and methods didn't have to change. Moving north or south into a new zone where conditions were different meant that people needed to invent new ways to farm. Invention takes time.

On a world map it is clear that the Americas and Africa stretch north-south and Eurasia spreads east-west. Farming began in the ideal growing conditions of the Fertile Crescent and spread rapidly east and west through similar conditions. For the people living in north–south oriented continents, farming took longer to catch on because methods and crops had to be adjusted to the differences in climate.

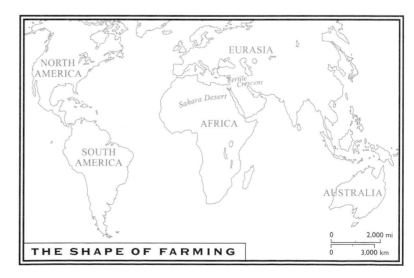

THE SHAPE OF FARMING

Images of a crocodile and other animals are cut into the rock at Messak Settafet, in the Sahara Desert. Scientists don't know how long ago the engravings were made, but you wouldn't find crocodiles there today.

BORN TO BE FREE

The penned sheep may have been tame, but they weren't bred by farmers either then or now. These were Barbary sheep. Barbary sheep are completely different animals from domestic sheep. They belong to a different genus—*Ammotragus*—which was not domesticated.

Parts of Europe were so different from the Fertile Crescent that it would take centuries for people to discover ways to work the new growing zones. Northern forests were horrible for herding, with harsh winters that made grazing almost impossible. The bitter winters killed off anything planted in the autumn—the planting season for the Fertile Crescent. The idea may seem simple, but it would take generations for people to discover that planting in the spring gave seedlings time to mature before the winter freeze.

The same climate barriers that slowed the spread of crops to the north and south slowed the spread of cattle, too. But, not all barriers have to do with climate changes. Something else stood in the way of African cattle—something so tiny that you wouldn't expect it to be able to stop herds of hulking cows, and yet it did. It was the tsetse fly. The tsetse fly is deadly to cattle. On the fringe of the African tropical forests, at the edge of what was then savannah, the tsetse flies swarmed, preventing cattle migration.

In the Sahara early foragers collected wild cereal grasses, sorghum, and millet. They hunted crocodile and antelope. And now it looks as if they herded Barbary sheep 1,000 or more years before they herded cattle. On the field trip our scholars examined very convincing evidence that these foragers had built stalls for their sheep. You don't build stalls for wild animals. These Saharan people must have tamed their sheep, but getting them into the enclosures would have been a challenge. One rock art picture the Prehistoric Society visited on their field trip shows a sheep running from dogs and hunters.

The pictures of daily life in the rock art showed that by 7,000 years ago people were herding domestic cattle, sheep (not Barbary sheep), and goats as well as hunting, fishing, and gathering plants. The rock art shows us what their relationship with animals must have been like: some scenes are of hunting animals, some scenes are of raising animals. There are carvings of giraffe, rhinoceros, elephant, buffalo, and crocodile from what scholars call the Big Game phase of life in the Sahara, perhaps 7,000–5,000 years ago. One carving shows hunters trapping ostriches and giraffes in stone enclosures. There are paintings of herders with their animals. There are even cow-milking scenes.

The Sahara began its shift to the desert it is today about 4,500 years ago. As the climate got drier and drier, herders had to move south in search of grasses for their animals. The wild growth of the savannah wasn't enough to feed the increasing population. People needed to boost food production. They began to farm. Some cereals such as sorghum and millet did well in the growing conditions south of the Sahara. Some cereals such as wheat and barley did not. In other areas of Africa where growing conditions were quite different, other crop combinations sprouted. In wet West Africa you might have farmed yams and African rice.

On the last evening of the Prehistoric Society's field trip in the Sahara, Graeme Barker and his company of scholars were doing a little foraging of their own. They'd lost their kitchen truck. They spent hours looking behind dune after dune. Life in the Sahara is still a challenge.

" Rock art, Wadi Teshuinat, Libya, probably between 7,000 and 3,000 years ago

WEIRD CROPS

Not all crops grown more than 3,000 years ago are familiar to us today. In Ethiopia farmers domesticated a cereal called *tef,* an oil named *noog,* and a banana whose fruit is not the part that you eat.

CHAPTER 23

WESTWARD, NO!
THE PEOPLING OF THE PACIFIC

The Kon Tiki *raft was made out of balsa wood. Thor Heyerdahl and his crew sailed this raft from Peru to the island of Raroia in Polynesia, a trip that took 101 days.*

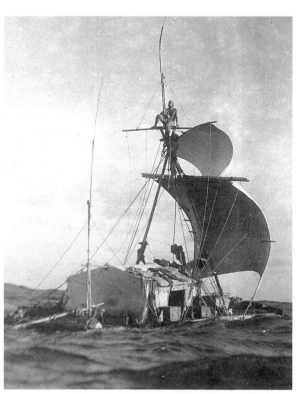

The balsa-wood raft floated over the top of the wave then dropped between swells and rose again. Explorer and archaeologist Thor Heyerdahl stood at the bow watching the sunset. *Kon-Tiki's* sail strained with the westerly trade winds. Was Heyerdahl scared when he looked into the heaving Pacific Ocean? Did those nine balsa logs lashed together with hemp rope appear puny in the embrace of all that water power? Did the cabin built in the middle, framed with bamboo canes, sided in woven reeds and roofed with overlapping banana leaves feel flimsy when the spray shot overhead? Heyerdahl must have been very determined to prove his point to risk his life and the lives of his crew of five. He would show the world. He would prove that it was possible that ancient Peruvians had courageously cast off into the Pacific Ocean more than 1,000 years ago and settled Polynesia.

Oh, experienced sailors had warned him. It will sink, they said. The balsa will soak up water like a sponge, then sink like a rock. The ropes will fray and snap under the strain the first week. But Thor Heyerdahl discovered something ancient seafarers must have known about seagoing rafts. He wrote an entry in his journal that would later appear in his book *Kon-Tiki*: "The round logs astern let the water pass as if through prongs of a fork. The advantage of a raft was obviously this: the more leaks the better—through the gaps in our floor the water ran out, but never in."

He'd been warned by an experienced explorer and scholar that "the task of science is investigation pure and simple. Not to try and prove this or that." But Heyerdahl didn't listen to that warning any more than he listened to the warnings about his raft. He *would* prove it was possible to raft westward to Polynesia from South America.

The scholar had argued, "none of the peoples of South America got over to the islands in the Pacific. Do you know why? The answer is simple enough. They couldn't have gotten there. They had no boats!"

Heyerdahl answered, "They had rafts.... You know, balsa-wood rafts."

Days had turned to weeks aboard the *Kon-Tiki*. Heyerdahl wrote in his journal, "It was easy to see that the balsa logs absorbed water.... I broke off a piece of the sodden wood and threw it over-board. It sank quietly beneath the surface and slowly vanished down into the depths." Would they make it to Polynesia? Had the ancient Peruvians? Heyerdahl admitted to the superior sailing abilities of the Polynesians. He knew their double canoes were sturdy yet nimble. Even their smaller canoes could carry 18,000 pounds. Families could travel from island to island in boats that were loaded with caged livestock—pigs and dogs and chickens and rats. Heyerdahl's Peruvian balsa raft was clumsy and impossible to steer in any direction other than with the wind.

Scholars would later discredit Heyerdahl's journey by pointing out that prehistoric Peruvians didn't use sails— they used paddles. Heyerdahl used sails. And the drawings and carvings of ancient South American watercraft showed rafts with only three logs, or two-person rafts made of bundled reeds, or inflated sealskin rafts—none as large as nine lashed logs—and none with

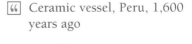
“ Ceramic vessel, Peru, 1,600 years ago

A man paddles a raft in the form of a supernatural fish. This pottery figurine found in Peru was a symbol of achievement that was buried with its owner.

Stowaway

Thor Heyerdahl may not have deliberately brought animals with him, as the ancient immigrants must have, but it appears there was one stowaway. Heyerdahl writes in Kon-Tiki,

"Aft, in a little hole by the steering block, lived a crab which was called Johannes and was quite tame.... Johannes sat...in his doorway with his eyes wide open, waiting for the change of watch. Every man who came on watch had a scrap of biscuit or a bit of fish for Johannes, and we only needed to stoop down over the hole for him to come right out on his doorstep and stretch out his hands. He took the scraps out of our fingers with his claws and ran back into the hole, where he sat down in the doorway and munched like a schoolboy cramming his food in his mouth."

sails—and no canoes at all. These small rafts were hardly designed for moving groups of people thousands of miles. Where would you put the supplies for a three- or four-month journey? And what about stowing away livestock and plants with which to begin a new life?

Heyerdahl could have argued that supplies weren't a problem. On their journey rain filled the water cans and the fish were plentiful—so plentiful that flying fish shot out of the water and flopped onto the deck. One landed right in the cook's frying pan! But Heyerdahl had no room on the *Kon-Tiki* for things to plant once they landed. The raft had no room for the things migrating people would bring with them from home—animals to breed, crops to plant.

Wherever they came from, the first explorers who settled the islands of Polynesia brought plants and animals. Thor Heyerdahl tried to support his theory of westward migration through the plants he found on the islands. He thought that the South Americans had brought the sweet potato, chili peppers, and cotton. He was sure that the bullrush plant he found growing in the crater swamps of Polynesia was the same as the bullrush that grew in Peru. Later, botanists discovered that some of the plants that Heyerdahl claimed the first settlers carried from South America had actually been growing on the islands thousands of years before any people arrived. Plants move from island to island in ways you might never suspect. Some seeds float their way to a new home. Others arrive by wind. Ferns spread their lightweight spores on the breeze. Some seeds travel via air-transport on birds' feet, in their feathers, or all wrapped up in a neat fertilized pellet—splat!

On the raft, Heyerdahl and his mates ran into foul weather: "the wind shook the bamboo wall and whistled and howled in all the rigging...." Nights were the worst: "As we lay there, each man on his straw mattress, we could feel the reed matting under us heaving in time with the wooden logs." It felt like they were "lying on the back of a large breathing animal." One night Heyerdahl woke up feeling uneasy. Something about the movement of the waves had changed. Within moments the raft shattered on a coral

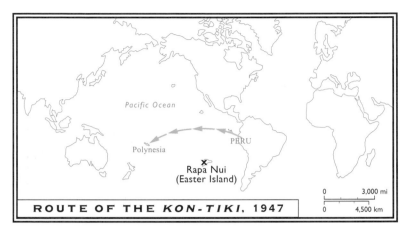

ROUTE OF THE *KON-TIKI*, 1947

While the Kon-Tiki sailed in the direction of these arrows from east to west, we now know that Polynesia was settled by people who journeyed across the Pacific from west to east.

reef. Thor Heyerdahl and his crew had made it to Polynesia on a balsa-wood raft.

Adventurers like Thor Heyerdahl don't sit still easily. The saltwater had probably not thoroughly dried on his skin before he set his sights for the most remote island of Polynesia—the island known to Polynesians as Te-Pito-o-te-Henua, which means "Navel of the World." The first European to set foot on the island landed on Easter Sunday in 1722 and named it Easter Island. The people who live there today call it Rapa Nui. Heyerdahl was convinced that Rapa Nui was first settled by Peruvians, not by island-hopping Polynesians. He'd proved that it was possible that they *could* have made the journey. Could he prove that they *did*?

As on most Polynesian islands, the majority of Rapa Nui's settlements were near the coast. Heyerdahl and other archaeologists studying foundations and the debris people had left behind determined that the houses were grouped in twos and threes alongside stone chicken houses and stone garden enclosures. Some people chose to live

[“] Stone house, Easter Island, Chile, 600–400 years ago

BREADCRUMBS

Plants aren't the only thing to leave a trail of evidence that allows scientists to follow the movement of people through Polynesia. They can observe the appearance of artifacts, such as the pottery that settlers bring with them when they move from place to place. One of the most recent trails of evidence scientists are following is human DNA. The DNA trail suggests a fairly recent eastward migration, perhaps stemming from Taiwan.

66 Stone fishhook, Easter Island, Chile, date unknown

farther away from the coast, where the soil was better and salt spray didn't kill the plants. Some houses were clustered around religious sites where ceremonies were performed on altarlike platforms. The curved houses nearest the sacred places were built with care for the priests and chiefs who held positions of respect among the people of the island. The best houses were built on cut-stone foundations. They looked like beehives with plant material tightly woven into the arched pole frame. To keep the cold and rain out, entrances were tiny. People had to crawl through the doorways. Most people lived in huge sleeping shelters built to hold as many as 200 people.

Each part of the island had its own specialty. If you lived on volcanic rock, you would work the obsidian. If you lived near a forest, you would cut down trees. If you lived on good soil, you might grow bananas. The groups traded with one another.

Heyerdahl needed some concrete evidence to identify the first people to arrive at Rapa Nui as Peruvians. He looked for things that were uncommon in other parts of Polynesia but could be found in Peru. He found bits and pieces, here and there— stone pillows, stone fishhooks, and bone needles. But nothing pointed to one group of people at one point in time from Peru who might have brought these items to Rapa Nui. Even the techniques that the natives in Rapa Nui used to make tools were not at all like the methods the Peruvians used. Heyerdahl should have listened to the scholar who told him that a scientist's job is not to try and force the evidence to prove a point. But Heyerdahl did not listen. Desperate for any solid proof, Heyerdahl turned his attention to the statues on Rapa Nui. Weren't they similar to statues in South America?

Like everyone who has seen them, Heyerdahl was awed by the statues on Rapa Nui. The Easter Island Heads, or *moai,* as they are known to the islanders, are each bigger and heavier than a school bus full of rocks tipped up on its end. Even the toppled statues appeared huge to Heyerdahl: "it is the head of a fallen giant...you can walk about freely on his chest and stomach, or stretch yourself out on his nose, which often is as long as an ordinary bed."

While peering into the crater where most of the statues had been quarried, Heyerdahl wondered how nearly a thousand years ago the workers had moved those massive stones out of the quarry and up onto the platforms where they stood all around the island. Legend says the statues walked. From the crater rim Heyerdahl studied the hollows in the steep clifflike walls where statues had been cut out long ago. The volcanic rock had a hard crust, but once the ancient carvers broke through, the stone inside was soft as chalk. One huge block remained still attached to the rock. The carvers must have given up when they realized that it was just too massive to move. At 65 feet, it would weigh at least 270 tons. Below Heyerdahl, hundreds of statues littered the crater floor in all stages of completion—some standing up,

" Statues, Easter Island, Chile, 1,000–500 years ago

These stone statues of ancient leaders, or moai, *on Easter Island have turned their backs to the sea for 550 years. They provided spiritual protection and reassurance to the people of the island.*

MY KINGDOM FOR A TREE

There was no lack of rock for carving the statues, but moving them required timber and rope—lots of it. As the demand for statues grew, so did the demand on the island's forests. There are just so many trees on an island. When the trees were gone, islanders could no longer build canoes. Without canoes, the islanders became trapped—stranded in the middle of the Pacific. They could no longer fish offshore. The communities that logged no longer had anything to trade, nor did the off-shore fisherman. As often happens, inequalities led to conflict.

others on their backs, many broken. No two looked exactly the same.

Heyerdahl learned from island legends and interviews with islanders that the carvers had been respected artists. The community paid them for their skills by taking care of them. They were relieved from day-to-day survival tasks and were free to pursue their art. Chiefs commissioned statues while they were living so that they would be remembered after they died. Competition was heated among the chiefs for who ranked highest and who deserved the biggest and the best statue. The carvers raced to make hundreds of statues.

It wasn't until after the person died that his statue was moved onto a platform, with the statue's back to the sea. Once the statue was raised, carvers hollowed out the eye sockets. Like a giant "on" switch, adding eyeballs activated the statue's *mana,* or spiritual power. But how did they move the statues out of the crater and onto the platforms? Heyerdahl had found a new obsession. Using round logs and lots of rope, he experimented. Taking his cue from the legends that said the statues "walked," Heyerdahl stood the statues upright and wiggled them forward by rocking them from side to side. The towering heads staggered forward. It was more of a waddle than a walk, but enough to convince Heyerdahl where the walking stories had started.

Heyerdahl hoped to prove that the statues were similar to statues in South America, but it was clear that the *moai* of Easter Island were more like statues throughout Polynesia, all springing from a shared belief system and shared customs. In the end the Easter Island Heads turned their backs on Heyerdahl's theory just as they turned their backs on the sea. Thor Heyerdahl was wrong about the direction from which the first settlers of the islands of the Pacific had come. He never did prove his theory. But science advanced with his courageous voyage on the *Kon-Tiki*—just not in the "direction" that he expected.

CHAPTER 24

MUTANT EARS TAKE OVER

THE ORIGINS OF FARMING IN THE AMERICAS

The world that Cristobal Colombo, a.k.a. Christopher Columbus, bungled his way into was so strange he called it the New World. The people were different. The animals were different. Even the plants were different.

Who had ever heard of an underground nut? (A peanut.)

And the red juicy berry, how on earth would you cook with that? (The tomato; the Italians obviously found ways.)

The potato was so bizarre to the Europeans that they thought it gave you leprosy.

Columbus had traveled to find spices and he wasn't about to go home empty-handed—even if these crops *did* look awfully strange. Chili peppers, he decided, were just the thing—a spice. (Chili peppers spread so quickly throughout the Old World that until recently botanists thought chili peppers had originated in India instead of South America.)

On each of his return trips to Spain, Columbus loaded his ships with seedlings and plants. The corn and beans transplanted well in the Old World. They were a lot like the cereal crops Europeans were familiar with—the wheat and barley and rye. So they spread quickly. Other plants were a bit of a curiosity. No one quite knew what to make of the pineapple. And chocolate? The damp cargo hold of the ship turned the cacao beans moldy. It's no wonder chocolate wasn't very popular in the Old World.

This Navajo woman shows off two plants farmed in the Americas today—corn and greenthread. Greenthread is used to make flavorful teas that have medicinal value. The corn has come a long way from its scrawny wild ancestor.

A FEW KERNELS

Corn is often called maize after its scientific name *Zea mays*. In Britain "corn" means cereals such as wheat and barley.

PLOWING THROUGH EUROPE

The plow seems to have been invented in Meso-potamia more than 5,000 years ago. As with many useful inventions it caught on and spread quickly. By 4,500 years ago the plow had spread throughout most of Europe.

And why was Columbus sailing to the Americas instead of Native Americans sailing to Europe? Why didn't Native Americans "discover" Spain? What was it about the European way of life that had people hopping into ships and setting out to discover new worlds? It all boils down to farming. What *was* it about agriculture in the Americas that made it so different from agriculture in the rest of the world? And how does the way you farm give rise to your way of life? To answer those questions, we must go back thousands of years before Columbus's voyage. We must go back to the beginnings of farming and see what made it different in the Americas.

One of the major differences was the domestication of animals. There were many large animals in Europe and Asia and Africa that were right for taming—cattle, sheep, goats, pigs, horses, and donkeys. Not only could farmers eat these large animals, but they could also make the wool and hides into everything from clothing to shelter. The animals provided transportation and they worked for the farmers. They were the tractors of the prehistoric world. They pulled plows and turned millstones to grind flour. And what dropped to the ground while the animals worked made great fertilizer.

Large animals increase crop production. They can till a field faster than a human, and the plows certainly can break up crusted, rocky topsoil better than a human toiling by hand. The Old World animals helped with threshing, grinding, and irrigation—all the while fertilizing away.

The large animals in the Americas that had survived the extinction at the end of the last Ice Age were not ideal for taming. Only two large animals, the llama and the alpaca, were domesticated in one small area of South America, high-altitude grasslands in the Andes. And even these animals had their limits. You couldn't ride them, and they wouldn't pull a cart or plow. Guinea pigs, turkeys, dogs, and ducks were also domesticated, but these few animals can't compare to all those tamed in the Old World.

Another difference in farming between the Old World and the New has to do with lifestyle. Do you move on after the harvest, or do you stay in one place and live off the same plot of land? In the Old World many early farming societies lived year round in one place. In the New World very few of the first farming societies stayed in one place. They moved with the seasons.

Guilá Naquitz Cave in the highlands of Mexico is a good example of this seasonal way of life in the Americas. Scientists can tell what time of year the cave was occupied by the plant remains found around the hearths. Small bands, perhaps extended families, lived there from August to December each year. They ate acorns, berries, and the seeds and fruits of thorny cactus. At first, only a small part of their diet came from the wild squash and bean plants that grew in the area. The families tended the wild squash seed beds. They watered and weeded and watched. They thinned the bed, pulling weeds and the smaller squash plants to make room for the heartiest squash. Over time this attention to the wild plants altered them so much that scientists no longer consider them wild. To date, this domesticated squash is the oldest evidence of farming in the Americas—as old as 10,000 years ago.

Native Americans had begun to farm, yet most stayed mobile. Five thousand years ago small family bands were still

Squash seed, Oaxaca, Mexico, 10,000 years ago

on the move, seasonally farming a very small percentage of what they ate. Although farming was widespread in the Americas, most of the land was still occupied by hunter-gatherers.

One of the plants that eventually spread throughout the Americas was corn. Corn's wild ancestor teosinte still grows in Mesoamerica. It doesn't look very much like the corn we're used to seeing. For one thing, it has no cob. It looks more like a giant wild grass. Native American farmers selected mutant teosinte plants. They chose plants with cobs—small cobs compared to what you are used to seeing in the supermarket—but cobs nonetheless. Over time the cob evolved from its original tiny fruit case to the large cob with lots of tightly packed kernels we eat today. Corn is a perfect example of artificial selection—where humans, not nature, select. In the case of corn, people chose the plants with larger cobs for easy picking. But the tightly packed seeds sprouted a mass of overcrowded seedlings. The seedlings choked one another out. What nature would have rejected, humans selected, but now domesticated corn had to be planted by human hand.

Hand planting is slow and labor intensive. In other parts of the world, farmers planted cereals easily just by scattering seed. In the Americas, the cob had to be picked by hand. Cereal farmers cut their crops with a sickle.

Cereal planting had speed and ease on its side. And when you farm, you feed more people, and when you feed more people your population is free to grow. With larger populations, villages grow into towns, which then grow into cities. When people grow more than their families can eat, they can trade the surplus. People are then free to specialize—to become artists, or toolmakers, or shipbuilders—and trade their skills for food. Soon you have adventurers setting out to discover new lands, filled with new things to trade.

Corn cobs have changed over the years. Teosinte, corn's wild ancestor, is on the left, and modern corn, like you find in a supermarket, is on the right.

Corn in the Americas may have had many drawbacks. It may have contributed to slow population growth, but it still spread from Mesoamerica through North America. In southeastern North America, communities experimented with strange alternatives—goosefoot, sunflowers, and marsh elder. If it hadn't been for those teosinte mutants, you might be eating goosefoot for breakfast.

So how *do* scientists know what prehistoric people ate? You may not want to know the answer—one way they learn is from paleofeces. Oh, yes. There are scientists dedicated to dung. They get their scoop from the poop, so to speak. There are even dung conferences where scientists talk about the digestive habits of ancient peoples—their paleo-diets. The old "you are what you eat" saying has truth to it, so it seems. And what goes in must come out. Does fecal matter? You bet. It reveals a lot about lifestyle and health.

Archaeologists have gathered hundreds of fecal samples that are more than 2,000 years old from places such as Hinds Cave in Texas. The rock shelters in this area are dry, protected environments perfect for preserving perishable materials such as baskets, mats, nets, sandals, wooden spears—and paleofeces. What scientists are finding in the paleofeces supports what they thought ancient lifestyles might be like—for example, the shift from large game to small game. Deer had once been the main source of protein for the people of Hinds Cave and is present in the early paleofeces. Over time, the content of the dung shifts to reflect a diet of smaller animals—rodents, rabbits, snakes, and birds.

What prehistoric people ate isn't the only information gained from studying paleofeces. Digested pollen tells scientists what time of year a particular site was occupied. Parasites tell a lot about the general health of the individuals. DNA tells which plants were farmed and which plants were foraged. And the feces themselves can be dated using a special offshoot of carbon dating.

Agriculture in the Americas may have gotten off to a slow start, but today these plants selected by the first American farmers feed over half the world. And the chocolate? Well, it seems people have acquired a taste for it after all.

Paleofeces, Texas, United States, more than 2,000 years

Paleofeces, such as this sample excavated at Hinds Cave in Texas, contain evidence of what ancient people ate.

CHAPTER 25

AN UNAUTHORIZED TRAVEL GUIDE TO NORTH AMERICA
COMPLEX SOCIETIES

Thinking of getting away from it all? If you were looking for a "happening" vacation destination in North America 1,000 years ago, you would have had a variety of fabulous choices. Which vacation package would you choose?

Cahokia, Illinois

Visit North America's largest city where the Mississippi, Missouri, and Illinois Rivers come together just eight miles from what will one day be St. Louis. Population 10–15,000 people (we can only guess since no one keeps records yet).

Accommodations: Live with the elite in five-star accommodations inside the city barricade. Don't let those scalps on the fence posts alarm you as you enter the city. As long as you keep the many layers of chiefs in Cahokia happy, you have nothing to worry about. Take up residence in any one of the clusters of small houses in and around the city. These

Downtown Cahokia's main attraction is Monk's Mound, the tallest prehistoric structure in what would one day become the United States. This reconstruction shows the thatchy roofed houses that were built inside and outside the town walls.

66 Building foundations, Cahokia, Illinois, United States, 1,000 years ago

Excavations at Cahokia reveal the dirt foundations of rectangular houses. These single-family homes were built in a well-planned formation around the central plaza.

family neighborhoods each have all the amenities—granary to store food, meetinghouse for those hard-to-make decisions, and, of course, the sweat lodge to help you chill out after your stressful day of carrying 70-pound baskets of dirt up the 10-story, flat-topped Monk's Mound built for the great chief of Cahokia. Nothing but the best for the town's most revered. (Traveler's Tip: The more tattoos the more important the chief.) Please be sure to extinguish all smoking materials before entering the city. The grass-thatched roofs are prone to burning, making everyone's stay less enjoyable.

What to eat: Don't miss the wide variety of corn dishes served up along with squash and beans. If you are a vegetarian, you've come to the right place—meat is not often on the menu. Brains are almost never offered as they are reserved to soften hides for clothing.

Things to do while in Cahokia: Come join area priests at Woodhenge to celebrate the longest day of the year at the Summer Solstice Sunrise Observance. Arrive early and watch astronomers tinker with the circle of red-cedar, telephone-pole-sized posts to get the alignments just right for premium sunrise viewing. If your visit coincides with an equinox, the sun rises directly over the head chief's residence atop

❝ Monk's Mound, Cahokia, Illinois, United States, about 1,000 years ago

❝ Storage pot, Cahokia, Illinois, United States, about 1,000 years ago

❝ Serpent Mound, Peebles, Ohio, United States, about 930 years ago

Monk's Mound, instilling awe and wonder... much oohing and ahhing. Free.

Shopping: Be sure to visit one of Cahokia's potters and watch distinctive pots being made. Area artisans kneeling on reed mats coil ropes of clay into pleasing shapes then smooth out the seams with round stones or chunks of gourd. Clay is gathered locally from streambeds, cleaned, then mixed with crushed mussel shell, limestone, and pieces of old crumbled pots.

Nearby attractions: Don't miss Serpent Mound. This quarter-mile-long serpent built from stones and clay slithers along a bluff in Ohio. What were the architects thinking? There are no human burials or artifacts in the mound. A work of art? Or a ceremonial center? You be the judge.

Knife River, North Dakota
Accommodations: Spacious summer accommodations that sleep 30 are located on terraces just above the Knife River. These

This earth lodge has been reconstructed at Knife River National Historic Site in North Dakota. Earth lodges are spacious homes—40 to 50 feet in diameter. People set up their living spaces along the inside walls; some lodges even had canopy beds.

earth lodges (owned and run by women) are built for comfort, with recessed dirt floors for warmth. The older units are rectangular, but recent renovations completed 500 years ago have domed roofs covered in turf. All views are southwest and outstanding. Locals love sitting on top of their houses, hanging out, and shooting the breeze. For your personal safety, smoke holes are covered to keep small children and dogs from falling through. Smaller winter accommodations are available on the low-lying forest, where they are shielded from icy winter winds.

Amenities: Available without extra cost is the use of the sweat lodge. This four-foot-high dome is constructed of bent willow branches and covered in bison hides. For your relaxation, hot stones are carried in on deer antlers and dropped into a hole dug in the center of the room. Sprinkling water on the stones provides a lovely steam-room atmosphere. While chanting and praying, sit naked on plump cushions stuffed with sweet smelling sage. The pipe is passed to all participants.

Getting around: Dogs do the heavy lifting around Knife River. Travois are harnessed to the dogs. These stick platforms are shaped like an **A** with the two ends dragging on the

A pile of smashed-up bison bones at Head-Smashed-In Buffalo Jump. Native Americans hunted bison here for about 5,500 years. We often call these animals buffalo, but their proper name is American bison (Bison bison).

“ Bison bones, Alberta, Canada, 5,500 to 200 years ago

ground. Travois tracks, like roadways, meander through the village. No tipping necessary.

By boat: Fishing is a must on your Knife River vacation. The river is loaded with walleyes, catfish, and sturgeon. Cup-shaped boats can be rented for a nominal fee. They are made from bison hides stretched over willow branches. (Everything here seems to be made from bison hide and willow branches. In fact, the name of the local tribe, the Hidatsa, means People of the Willows.)

What to wear: Casual attire for most occasions. Women, be sure to bring your dresses of deerskin and leggings that run from ankles to knees. Comfortable deerskin moccasins for walking (remove deer fur first, please) are a must. Don't forget your necklace of mussel shells and you are ready to go anywhere.

Nearby attractions: In Alberta, Canada, join the party at Head-Smashed-In Buffalo Jump. Here you can see a waterfall of bellowing brown bison leap to their deaths as hundreds of local hunters stampede them over cliffs. The flies and the stench are unforgettable as the butchering continues for days. Take home pemmican as a souvenir. Not unlike beef jerky, this tasty mashed and dried meat treat will stay fresh for months (also available in chokeberry flavor).

Before you go: When planning your trip to the Great Plains region it's wise to check ahead to find out who is currently in charge. Chiefs change often. Each village has its own all-purpose chief, but there is also a chief of the hunt, a war chief, a peacetime chief, and so on. Be sure to fill out your customer satisfaction survey on departure. Chiefs are rated according to popularity and your opinion is important.

Ozette, Washington

Enjoy sea breezes from this cape that juts out into the Pacific Ocean. Shorelines protected by a barrier reef make putting in your canoe simple here, unlike other areas along the coast. Great for the whole family.

Accommodations: No frills armylike barracks are the only accommodations available in this seacoast town. Houses are the size of tennis courts, sleeping many families. The shed-roofed buildings are made from cedar planks, surrounded by whale bones to redirect the rain water.

Getting around: Boating is a must while at Ozette. Sit with seven others in canoes made from giant hollowed-out cedar logs. Watch boatbuilders craft these canoes right on the beach. They begin by carving the bottom, then flip them over to hollow out the inside. To soften the wood and force the sides wider, they flood the canoe and heat the water by adding hot rocks. Finally the canoe is sanded smooth with sharkskin.

What to wear: Skirts of shredded cedar bark are all the rage. Men, be sure to pack your robes made from sea otter skins. Footwear optional. Accessorize with rings through your nose, necklaces, headbands, and bracelets (both men and women). Be sure to pack powdered hemlock to kill head lice.

Things to do while in Ozette: Book your whaling adventure early. Limited availability. Traditionally, whale hunts are restricted to the wealthiest families who have inherited whaling privileges. Come early as lengthy spiritual preparation is a must. Getting ready for one of these hunts makes training for a triathlon look easy. Join the fun while whalers

MUD PACK

A mudslide encased Ozette in an airtight, waterproof seal, preserving items that would normally rot in the moist air. In 1970 a winter storm eroded the banks, revealing the ancient village.

Harpoon, Ozette,
Washington, United States,
500 years ago

Fishermen used this harpoon head to hunt whales in Ozette, Washington. The harpoon blade is made from a mussel shell.

paddle with the humpbacks. When a whaler harpoons one, hold on for dear life. Keep those fingers crossed that the whale does not head out to sea. Sealskin floats are tied to the harpoons in hopes of tiring the whale. Once the whale has sufficiently tired, the canoe is pulled alongside where a boatman cuts the tendons of the flukes so the whale can't swim. One lucky individual gets to jump in the water with the whale and sew its mouth shut so that trapped gasses will keep it floating until they can tow it into shore. One sure way to book your reservation is to volunteer for this great opportunity to swim with the whales. Warning to wives of whalers: plan on spending your vacation napping. Whale hunting is taken *very* seriously in Ozette, and wives of whalers are not allowed out of bed until their husbands return with a whale.

Travel tip: While in Ozette, be sure to attend a potlatch dinner. Local chiefs pass out presents in celebration of their place in the community. Great place to get free stuff.

Bon voyage!

PUZZLING OVER THE PAST

Piecing together the story of our beginnings is a lot like trying to do a giant jumble without all the letters.

Will we ever discover all the missing pieces?

No.

Will we ever know with 100 percent certainty what actually happened?

No.

Foturnately it is pssobile to unredtsand the sotry eevn wehn the ltteers are mxied up.

When you use that big brain, you won't always get it right, but being human is all about risking getting it wrong. It's who we are. And sometimes we *do* get it right. From the first hominid who stood on two feet to those who dared push off their canoes into open sea, from the first human who uttered a word to those who communicated to all of us by crawling through underground tunnels into caves and illustrating their world, curious, innovative humans planted seeds, tamed animals, and changed the world. Go out and question. Take a chance. It's your destiny.

Lif'se a pzluze; ptu in a pecie.

> "I think and think for months and years, ninety-nine times, the conclusion is false. The hundredth time I am right."
>
> **—Physicist Albert Einstein**

TIMELINE

When writing about events that happened hundreds of thousands, and even millions of years ago, all dates are approximate.

5.5 million years ago
Earliest hominids (*Ardipithecus ramidus kadabba*) live in what is now the country of Ethiopia

3.6 million years ago
Early hominids leave footprints at Laetoli, Tanzania

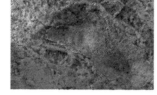

3.18 million years ago
Lucy (*Australopithecus afarensis*) lives and dies at Hadar, Ethiopia

2.5 million years ago
First use of stone tools and earliest members of the genus *Homo Australopithecus garhi* in East Africa

1.8 million years ago
Earliest occupation of Olduvai Gorge, Tanzania

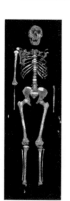

1.75 million years ago
Earliest hominids live outside Africa, at Dmanisi, Georgia

1.6 million years ago
Turkana Boy (*Homo erectus*) lives and dies in Kenya

1.25 million years ago
Earliest probable use of fire at Swartkrans, South Africa

800,000 years ago
Homo erectus reaches the Island of Flores, Indonesia, by boat; Gran Dolina Boy (*Homo antecessor*) lives and dies in Spain; earliest evidence of cannibalism at Gran Dolina, Spain

500,000–400,000 years ago
Earliest big-game hunting, Boxgrove, England; *Homo erectus* lives at the Zhoukoudian Cave, China

300,000 years ago
Many *Homo heidelbergensis* are buried in the Pit of Bones, at Atapuerca, Spain

120,000–70,000 years ago
Some of the earliest modern humans live and die at Klasies River Mouth, South Africa

50,000 years ago
Many Neandertals are buried at Shanidar Cave, Iraq

More than 40,000 years ago
People settle in Australia for the first time

40,000–12,000 years ago
Many Ice-Age animals die in the tar pits at La Brea, California

32,000 years ago
People paint and engrave some of the world's first art at Chauvet Cave, France

30,000 years ago
People first settle on the Solomon Islands

27,000 years ago
People build mammoth bone shelters, weave clothing, and make ceramic figures, at Dolní Věstonice, Czech Republic

25,000 years ago
The Kid, a Neandertal–modern human hybrid or a modern human child, lives and dies in the Lapedo Valley, Portugal

More than 12,000 years ago
People first enter the Americas

11,000 years ago
People of the Clovis culture hunt big and small game and gather plant foods across North America

10,400–7,800 years ago
First farmers at Abu Hureyra, Syria, and elsewhere in the Fertile Crescent of Southwest Asia

10,000 years ago
End of the last Ice Age; megafauna becomes extinct; earliest domesticated plants in Mesoamerica

9,300–8,100 years ago
People live at Çatalhöyük, Turkey

9,000 years ago
People keep Barbary sheep in pens and caves in the Sahara

8,500 years ago
People live seasonally at Koster, Illinois, site of North America's oldest cemetery

8,400 years ago
Kennewick Man dies in the United States

7,600 years ago
The Mediterranean Sea floods Lake Euxine and creates the Black Sea; people live year round at Koster, Illinois

7,000 years ago
People herd domestic cattle, sheep, and goats in the Sahara

6,300 years ago
Earliest known maize (corn) cobs harvested in Mexico

6,000 or more years ago
Farming and domestication of llamas and alpacas begins in South America

5,700–150 years ago
Native Americans stampede bison off the cliffs at Head-Smashed-In, Canada

5,500 years ago
The first cities develop in Mesopotamia (modern-day Iraq)

5,300 years ago
Ötzi the Iceman is killed in the Alps

5,000–3,500 years ago
Various episodes of building and use of Stonehenge, England

4,500 years ago
People in eastern North America cultivate sunflowers, gourds, and other plants; Sahara Desert becomes very dry; farming spreads south of the Sahara

This is one of several possible family trees of human evolution. The numbers in the bars are estimates of how many different hominids (not how many individual fossil bones) of each species have been found. For example, paleoanthropologists have discovered 11 fossil bones and teeth of Ardipithecus ramidus kadabba, which must belong to at least 5 different individuals.

4,300 years ago
Beginning of the Bronze Age in Europe; the Amesbury Archer is buried near Stonehenge, England

4,000–3,500 years ago
People introduce corn into southwestern United States from Mexico

1,400–1,200 years ago
First peopling of Easter Island (Rapa Nui) and Hawaii

1,000 years ago
Native American peoples live in villages beside the Knife River in North Dakota; people settle in New Zealand for the first time

1,000–750 years ago
As many as 15,000 people live in a city at Cahokia, Illinois

930 years ago
Native Americans build Serpent Mound in Ohio

500 years ago
Makah Indians occupy the village of Ozette, Washington, until it is buried by a mudslide; remains of wooden houses, canoes, and other items uncovered by erosion in 1970

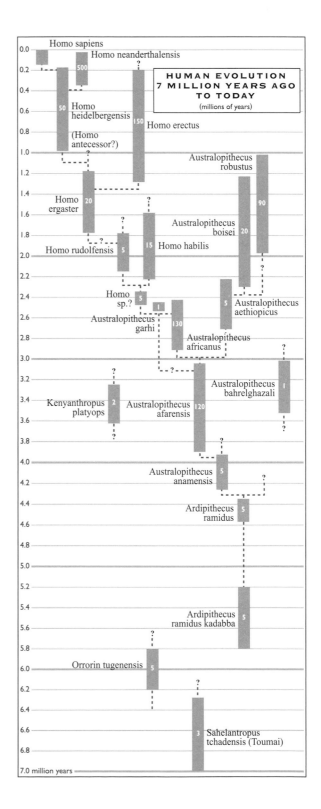

HUMAN EVOLUTION
7 MILLION YEARS AGO
TO TODAY
(millions of years)

FURTHER READING

Entries with 🔊 *indicate primary source material.*

GENERAL WORKS ON THE EARLY HUMAN WORLD

Bailey, Jill, and Tony Seddon. *The Young Oxford Book of the Prehistoric World.* New York: Oxford University Press, 1996.

Bryson, Bill. *A Short History of Nearly Everything.* New York: Broadway, 2003.

🔊 Darwin, Charles. *The Descent of Man*, reprint, 2nd ed. Amherst, N.Y.: Prometheus, 1998.

🔊 Darwin, Charles. *The Expressions of Emotions in Man and Animals.* reprint. New York: St. Martin's, 1979.

Fagan, Brian M. *People of the Earth: An Introduction to World Prehistory*, 11th ed. Upper Saddle River, N.J.: Pearson, 2004.

Foley, Robert. *Humans before Humanity: An Evolutionary Perspective.* Cambridge, Mass.: Blackwell, 1995.

Gowlett, John. *Ascent to Civilization: The Archaeology of Early Humans.* 2nd ed. New York: McGraw Hill, 1993.

Leakey, Richard, and Roger Lewin. *Origins Reconsidered: In Search of What Makes Us Human.* New York: Doubleday, 1992.

McKie, Robin. *Dawn of Man; The Story of Human Evolution.* New York: Dorling Kindersley, 2000.

Redfern, Martin. *The Kingfisher's Young People's Guide to the Planet Earth.* New York: Kingfisher, 1999.

Tattersall, Ian. *Becoming Human: Evolution and Human Uniqueness.* New York: Harcourt Brace, 1998.

———. *The Fossil Trail: How We Know What We Think We Know Human Evolution.* New York: Oxford University Press, 1996.

Wenke, Robert J. *Patterns in Prehistory: Humankind's First Three Million Years.* 4th ed. New York: Oxford University Press, 1999.

ATLASES

Aston, Mick, and Tim Taylor. *The Atlas of Archaeology.* New York: DK, 1998.

Bahn, Paul G. *The Atlas of World Archaeology.* New York: Checkmark, 2000.

Rollin, Sue. *The Illustrated Atlas of Archaeology.* New York: Warwick, 1982.

DICTIONARIES AND ENCYCLOPEDIAS

Darvill, Timothy. *The Concise Oxford Dictionary of Archaeology.* New York: Oxford University Press, 2002.

Delson, Eric, Ian Tattersall, Alison S. Brooks, and John S. Van Couvering. *Encyclopedia of Evolution and Prehistory*, 2nd ed. New York: Garland, 2000.

Jones, Steve, Robert Martin, and David Pilbeam, eds. *The Cambridge Encyclopedia of Human Evolution.* Cambridge, England: Cambridge University Press, 1992.

Vogel, J. O., ed. *Encyclopedia of Precolonial Africa.* Walnut Creek, Calif.: AltaMira, 1997.

BIOGRAPHY AND AUTOBIOGRAPHY

Fagan, Brian. *Archaeologists: Explorers of the Human Past.* New York: Oxford University Press, 2003.

Goodall, Jane. *My Life with the Chimpanzees.* New York: Pocket, 1996.

Heiligman, Deborah. *Mary Leakey: In Search of Human Beginnings.* New York: W. H. Freeman, 1995.

Leakey, Mary. *Disclosing the Past.* Garden City, N.Y.: Doubleday, 1984.

Morell, Virginia. *Ancestral Passions: The Leakey Family and the Quest for Humankind's Beginnings.* New York: Simon & Schuster, 1995.

Poynter, Margaret. *The Leakeys: Uncovering the Origins of Humankind.* Springfield, N.J.: Enslow, 1997.

Quackenbush, Robert M. *The Beagle and Mr. Flycatcher: A Story of Charles Darwin.* Englewood Cliffs, N.J.: Prentice-Hall, 1983.

Sis, Peter. *Tree of Life: Charles Darwin.* New York: Farrar Straus & Giroux, 2003.

Stefoff, Rebecca. *Charles Darwin and the Evolution Revolution.* New York: Oxford University Press, 1996.

AFRICA

Lewin, Roger. *The Origin of Modern Humans.* New York: Scientific American Library-W.H. Freeman, 1993.

Stringer, Christopher, and Robin McKie. *African Exodus: The Origins of Modern Humanity.* New York: Henry Holt, 1997.

AMERICAS

Dillehay, Thomas. *The Settlement of the Americas: A New Prehistory.* New York: Basic, 2000.

Nelson, Ted W., and Sharlene P. Nelson. *The Makah.* London: Franklin Watts, 2003.

Pauketat, Timothy R., and Nancy Stone Bernard. *Cahokia Mounds.* New York: Oxford University Press, 2003.

Sattler, Helen Roney. *The Earliest Americans.* New York: Clarion, 1993.

Struever, Stuart, and Felicia Antonelli Holton. *Koster: Americans in Search of Their Prehistoric Past.* Garden City, N.Y.: Doubleday, 1979.

ARCHAEOLOGY

Fagan, Brian M., ed. *The Oxford Companion to Archaeology.* New York: Oxford University Press, 1996.

McIntosh, Jane. *Archaeology.* New York: Knopf, 1994.

Orna-Ornstein, John. *Archaeology: Discovering the Past.* New York: Oxford University Press, 2002

Pitts, Michael, and Mark Roberts. *Fairweather Eden: Life Half a Million Years Ago as Revealed by the Excavations at Boxgrove.* London: Century, 1997.

Pringle, Heather. "New Women of the Ice Age." *Discover* (April 1998): 62–69.

Schick, Kathy D., and Nicholas Toth. *Making Silent Stones Speak.* New York: Simon & Schuster, 1993.

AUSTRALIA AND THE PACIFIC

Flenley, John, and Paul Bahn. *The Enigmas of Easter Island.* New York: Oxford University Press, 2003.

Heyerdahl, Thor. *Kon-Tiki: Across the Pacific by Raft.* New York: Franklin Watts, 1950.

Mulvaney, John, and Johan Kamminga. *The Prehistory of Australia.* Washington, D.C.: Smithsonian Institution Press, 1999.

Thomas, W. E. *Some Myths and Legends of the Australian Aborigines.* London: Whitcombe & Tombs, 1923.

CAVE ART

Bahn, Paul, and Jean Vertut. *Journey through the Ice Age.* Berkeley: University of California Press, 1997.

Chauvet, Jean-Marie, Eliette Brunel Deschamps, and Christian Hillaire. *Dawn of Art: The Chauvet Cave.* New York: Abrams, 1996.

Lauber, Patricia. *Painters of the Cave.* Washington, D.C.: National Geographic, 1998.

CHIMPANZEES

de Waal, Frans. *Peacemaking among Primates.* Cambridge, Mass.: Harvard University Press, 1989.

Goodall, Jane. *Chimps.* New York: Aladdin, 1989.

Savage-Rumbaugh, Sue, and Roger Lewin. *Kanzi: The Ape at the Brink of the Human Mind.* New York: Wiley, 1994.

EARLY HOMINIDS

Johanson, Donald, and Maitland Edey. *Lucy: The Beginnings of Humankind.* New York: Simon & Schuster, 1981.

Johanson, Donald C., and Kevin O'Farrell. *Journey from the Dawn: Life with the World's First Family.* New York: Villard, 1990.

Lewin, Roger. *Bones of Contention: Controversies in the Search for Human Origins.* New York: Simon & Schuster, 1987.

Picq, Pascal, and Nicole Verrechia. *Lucy and Her Times.* New York: Henry Holt, 1999.

Walker, Alan, and Pat Shipman. *The Wisdom of the Bones: In Search of Human Origins.* New York: Knopf, 1996.

Wilkinson, Philip, ed. *Early Humans.* New York: Knopf, 1989.

FARMING

Balter, Micheal. "The First Cities: Why Settle Down? The Mystery of Communities." *Science Magazine* (November 20, 1998).

Diamond, Jared. *Guns, Germs, and Steel: The Fates of Human Societies.* New York: W. W. Norton, 1999.

Patent, Dorothy Hinshaw. *Secrets of the Ice Man.* New York: Benchmark, 1998.

Woods, Michael, and Mary Woods. *Ancient Agriculture: From Foraging to Farming.* Minneapolis: Runestone, 2000.

FOSSILS

Busbey, III, Arthur B. *The Nature Companions Rocks, Fossils and Dinosaurs.* San Francisco: Fog City, 2002.

Parker, Steve, and Jane Parker. *Collecting Fossils: Hold Prehistory in the Palm of Your Hand.* New York: Sterling, 1997.

Taylor, Paul D. *Eyewitness: Fossil.* New York: Knopf, 1990.

Walker, Cyril. *Fossils.* New York: Dorling Kindersley, 2002.

NEANDERTALS

Shreeve, James. *The Neandertal Enigma: Solving the Mystery of Modern Human Origins.* New York: Morrow, 1995.

Solecki, Ralph. *Shanidar: The First Flower People.* New York: Knopf, 1971.

Trinkaus, Erik, and Pat Shipman. *The Neandertals: Changing the Image of Mankind.* New York: Knopf, 1993.

WEBSITES

The Amesbury Archer
www.wessexarch.co.uk/projects/amesbury/
archer.html
Archaeologists from Wessex Archaeology discover the grave of the Amesbury Archer.

Archaeology
www.archaeology.org/magazine.php?page=
online/news/human
The Archaeological Institute of America's story covering the discovery of *Australopithecus garhi.*

Ardipithecus ramidus kadabba Discovery
*www.berkeley.edu/news/berkeleyan/2001/07/11_*
homin.html
www.washingtonpost.com/ac2/wp-dyn/A47640-
2001Jul11
http://news.nationalgeographic.com/news/2001/
07/0712_ethiopianbones.html
News stories covering the discovery in Ethiopia of our earliest known ancestor.

The Arnhem Zoo Chimpanzee Colony
http://chimpansee.homestead.com/arnhemzoo.html
A guide to the life of the chimpanzees at Burgers' Zoo (the official name of the Arnhem Zoo).

Becoming Human
www.becominghuman.org/
An interactive journey through 4 million years of human evolution.

Cahokia Mounds State Historic Site
http://medicine.wustl.edu/~mckinney/cahokia/
cahokia.html
Discover Cahokia, the largest pre-Columbian settlement in North America.

Çatalhöyük: Excavations of a Neolithic Anatolian Höyük
http://catal.arch.cam.ac.uk/index.html
Read the diary entries written by the archaeologists who excavated the site.

The Cave of Chauvet-Pont-D'Arc
www.culture.gouv.fr/culture/arcnat/chauvet/en/
Offers tour of Chauvet Cave.

Dmanisi
www.dmanisi.org.ge
News, photos, and information on the oldest hominid site outside of Africa.

The First Europeans: Treasures from the Hills of Atapuerca
www.amnh.org/exhibitions/atapuerca
Features Atapuerca and the movement of *Homo erectus* out of Africa.

First Farmers
http://whyfiles.org/122ancient_ag/index.html
Shoulder your flint hoe, grab your digging stick, and discover the origins of domestication.

Head-Smashed-In Buffalo Jump
www.head-smashed-in.com
Learn about the Blackfoot Indians and how they hunted bison by running them off a cliff.

Human Evolution: You Try It
www.pbs.org/wgbh/aso/tryit/evolution
Learn about the Laetoli footprints, the Leakey family, and more.

The Jane Goodall Institute
www.janegoodall.org
Loads of information on Jane Goodall and chimpanzees.

Kanzi
www.gsu.edu/~wwwlrc/biographies/kanzi.html
The biography of Kanzi, the toolmaking bonobo.

Kennewick Man Virtual Interpretive Center
www.kennewick-man.com
The discovery, investigation, and legal battles surrounding Kennewick Man.

Knife River Indian Villages National Historic Site
www.nps.gov/knri/overview.htm
Explore an earth lodge, go hunting, and learn about Indian life in North Dakota's past.

The Leakey Foundation
www.leakeyfoundation.org
Biographical information on Mary Leakey and her work at Olduvai and elsewhere.

Makah Research Page
www.learningspace.org/instruct/jr_high/projects/ bgilbert/makah.htm
Follow a seventh-grade class as they learn about the buried village of Ozette and about the Makah Indian nation.

Minnesota State University Museum
www.mnsu.edu/emuseum/index.shtml
Online museum of anthropology, archaeology, prehistory, and history.

Mummy Tombs
www.mummytombs.com/mummylocator/ featured/otzi.htm
Information and student activities about the Iceman.

The Mysteries of Çatalhöyük
www.smm.org/catal
Read comics, play games, make a Neolithic dinner, and more.

National Museum of Natural History
www.mnh.si.edu
Visit an excavation in Kenya and examine the hominids in the Hall of Human Ancestors.

Page Museum
www.tarpits.org
Have an Ice-Age adventure as you explore the La Brea tar pits.

Past
www.ucl.ac.uk/prehistoric/past/
The Prehistoric Society's newsletter, which includes the society's field trip to the Sahara Desert.

Riddle of the Bones
www.pbs.org/wgbh/evolution/humans/riddle/ index.html
Learn from the bones of our ancestors and see the species that came before us in the "origins of humankind."

Secrets of Lost Empires
www.pbs.org/wgbh/nova/lostempires/easter
All you ever wanted to know about Easter Island and its stone statues.

Stone Pages
www.stonepages.com
Photos, information, and news about Stonehenge and many other European archaeological sites made of stone.

The Talk Origins Archive
www.talkorigins.org
Explores the creation versus evolution controversy.

Walking with Cavemen
www.bbc.co.uk/science/cavemen
Interactive games and lots of information on human ancestors, including Neandertals.

INDEX

PRIMARY SOURCE TEXT CREDITS

P. 27: Darwin, Charles. *The Descent of Man*, reprint, 2nd ed. Amherst, N.Y.: Prometheus, 1998, 632.

P. 29: Darwin, Charles. *The Expression of Emotions in Man and Animals*, reprint. New York: St. Martin's, 1979, 201.

PICTURE CREDITS

PETER ROBERTSHAW is an archaeologist and professor of anthropology at California State University, San Bernardino. After growing up in the north of England, he studied archaeology at Cambridge University, doing field research for his doctoral degree in South Africa. Later he moved to East Africa, where he excavated archaeological sites that provided information about the spread of farming and the rise of kingdoms. Since coming to California, he has returned regularly to Uganda to study the archaeology and history of the last thousand years. His research has been supported by the National Science Foundation, the National Geographic Society, and the National Endowment for the Humanities. He received the Outstanding Professor award from his university in 2002, and he has won both university and civic awards for his teaching. His books include *Early Pastoralists of Southwestern Kenya* and *A History of African Archaeology*. He has also written more than 70 articles and book chapters.

JILL RUBALCABA still isn't sure what she wants to be if she ever grows up. Writing lets her try on different hats, if only in her imagination. She began her working life as a college- and high-school mathematics teacher, all the while continuing to go to school to study more math, writing, and business. Later she worked as an engineer on the Patriot Missile. Ms. Rubalcaba is grateful to her children, Kelly and Dan, for showing her the joys of writing for children. She says, "The only thrill greater than losing myself in another world through reading is the thrill of losing myself in another world through writing." While writing this book, and imagining being a paleoanthropologist, Ms. Rubalcaba lived in Kennebunk, Maine, with her family and their cat, Scribbles. Although she moves nearly every three years and likes to "try on" different professions along with different locations, Ms. Rubalcaba hopes *always* to be a student.

RONALD MELLOR, who is professor of history at UCLA, first became enthralled with ancient history as a student at Regis High School in New York City. He is the statewide faculty advisor of the California History–Social Science Project (CHSSP), which brings university faculty together with K-12 teachers at sites throughout California. In 2000, the American Historical Association awarded the CHSSP the Albert J. Beveridge Award for K-12 teaching. Professor Mellor has held fellowships from the National Endowment for the Humanities and the American Council of Learned Societies. His research has centered on ancient religion and Roman historiography. His books include *Theia Rhome: The Goddess Roma in the Greek World*, *From Augustus to Nero: The First Dynasty of Imperial Rome*, *Tacitus*, *Tacitus: The Classical Heritage*, *The Historians of Ancient Rome*, *The Roman Historians*, and *The Ancient Roman World*.

AMANDA PODANY is a specialist in the history of the Ancient Near East and a professor of history at California State Polytechnic University, Pomona. She has taught there since 1990 and is currently serving as the director of the university's honors program. From 1993 to 1997 she was executive director of the California History–Social Science Project, a professional development program for history–social science teachers at all grade levels. Her work in professional development for teachers has received major grants from the California Postsecondary Education Commission and the United States Department of Education. Her publications include *The Land of Hana: Kings, Chronology, Scribal Tradition*, and *The Ancient Near Eastern World*. Professor Podany has also published numerous journal articles on ancient Near Eastern history and on approaches to teaching. She lives in Los Angeles with her husband and two children.

ACKNOWLEDGMENTS

Every book is a cooperative effort. This one is no exception. We are indebted to the following people for their thoughtful, generous, and enthusiastic contributions:

Ofer Bar-Yosef, Diane Brooks, Kathy Cruz-Uribe, Karen Fein, George Forrest, Richard Glass, Yohannes Haile-Selassie, Nancy Hirsch, Bob Hores, Janielle Keith, Ginger Knowlton, Marni McGee, Ronald Mellor, Wes Niewoehner, Amanda Podany, Denyse Robertshaw, Dan Rubalcaba, Kelly Rubalcaba, Ann Schulz, Linda Stockham, Stuart Sumida, Nancy Toff, Alan Walker, Jim Wheeler, and Stephen Wroe. Special thanks to the teachers and to the students whose creative input made for a better book.